The Drunkard's Son

A Chicago Story
Part Memoir, Part Not

By Dennis Foley

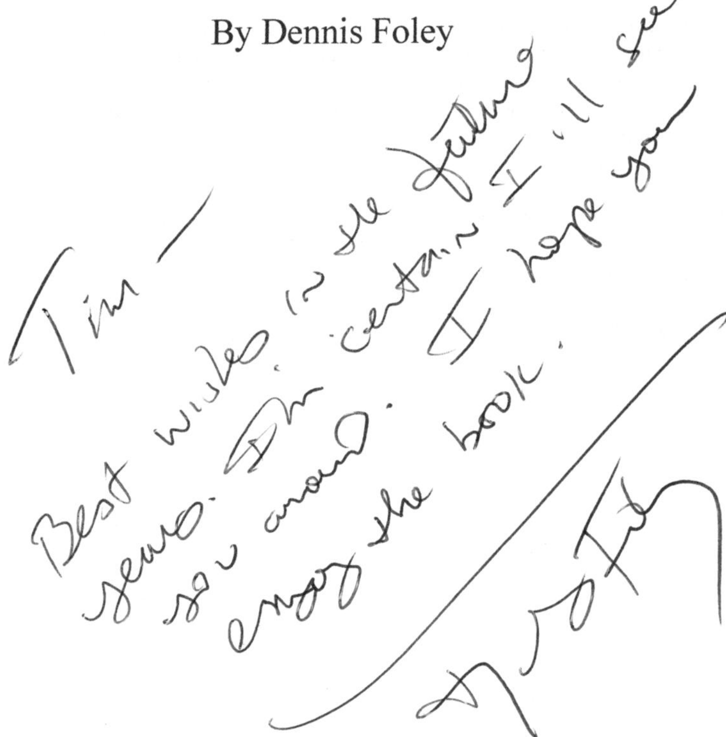

A SIDE STREET PRESS BOOK
Published by
Side Street Press Inc.
P.O. Box 438518
Chicago, IL 60643-8518

ISBN: 978-0-615-57862-0

Printed in the United States of America

First Edition: May 2012

AUTHOR'S NOTE

The names and other identifying details of some of the major and minor characters have been changed to protect individual privacy and anonymity. This book is part memoir, part fiction.

For my mother Josephine, the strongest person I have ever known, and for my bride Sue, whose love and support allow me to continue to chase dreams.

ACKNOWLEDGEMENT

Thanks to the following people who lent their eyes as readers of the manuscript: Denny Freyer, John Jakocko, Kevin Mc-Guire, Joe Mueller, and Sue Foley. Your thoughts, suggestions, edits, corrections, and time are truly appreciated.

Table of Contents

Holy Cross Hospital--Day 2 1
Popp's Tavern 5
Batman 12
Holy Cross Hospital--Day 3 18
Christmas, 1965 20
Mike, the Cat 22
Willie and Winston 27
Mr. O'Brien 35
Holy Cross Hospital--Day 4 45
The Snow of '67 47
Five Quarters 49
Naked Ladies 54
The Fish House 56
Sex 60
Holy Cross Hospital--Day 5 66
Brothers and Sisters 68
Fire 70
Haircuts 76
Darts 79
Holy Cross Hospital--Day 6 92
The Roach Motel 95
The Sanitarium 98
Father Mac 104
Dad's Place 110
Holy Cross Hospital--Day 7 114
Peaches 117
Coupons 125
Dark Side of the Moon 131
Public School 134
Holy Cross Hospital--Day 8 138
Mr. Brunner's House 140
Foot Rub 145
Holding Hands 148
The Black Limousine 151
Holy Cross Hospital--Day 9 159
Green White and Orange 161
Like Fathers--Like Sons 167
Sausage and Eggs 171
Breakfast With Dad 177
Holy Cross Hospital--Day 10 185

Holy Cross Hospital--Day 2

They have me tied down to this bed, blinding white sheets wrapped across my body. I feel like a tortured slave, each one of my limbs bound to the bed rail. But I can't complain too much. I'm the one who suggested they tie me down. "I'll rip this thing right outta me," I screamed when I came to after the operation. They had sewed a tube into my chest, beneath my left armpit. "First chance I get, it's gone." So, they put the ropes to me. Imagine that. Someone finally listened to what a fifteen-year-old had to say. Modern medicine at its finest.

I look kinda like Jesus on the cross with my arms stretched to my sides and all, cept I got a mattress beneath my back instead of a chunk of wood, and my legs are spread wide almost to a half-splits position, rather than danglin straight down like the son of man. But Jesus never had no tube runnin out the side of his chest. We both know that. The tube is drainin blood from my left lung. Now I know this might sound weird, but I actually like watchin my blood swim through that tube. I especially like when the chunks of flem-looking, bloody goobers wrestle their way through. I can see it all. The tube is made of a clear, flexible, plastic material and it's about a half-inch in diameter. Diameter--now there's a nice word. I learned all about that in geometry class this year. Talk about a class that'll put you to sleep. Geometry's the one. Sometimes the fluid races through that tube, other times it drags along like a lowly snail. But everything that goes through that tube is comin from me, from deep inside me--deep where my dreams hide.

I can't tell ya nothin 'bout my first day here. I was out cold when my buddies put me in a car and drove me in. That's why I started with Day 2. I'll tell ya this, though. My side is still killin me. In fact, my whole body is killin me. That's what a knife in the back will do to ya. But I'm out of danger now. Least that's what the doctors are sayin. They say I'm gonna make it. Still, I have to stay in this Intensive Care Unit just in case, they say, just in case.

There aint much to do in a hospital bed cept look around and think, and I'm getting tired of lookin around. There's six beds in here but only two are bein put to use. There's an old guy right across from me but he aint much to look at. His pencil face is covered over with whisker stubble and he's got an oxygen mask covering his mouth and nose. The rest of him is all covered over in sheets, just like me. He's alert though. He's been watchin me since I came to. His eyes squint to see around that oxygen mask. The old guy's not giving me a mean stare, though. Nope. His stare is caring, so I just stare right back at him. We haven't exchanged any chit-chat yet, but I feel like we're transferring words through some higher form of communication. That's the truth. It's either that, or it's the painkillers they're givin me. The old man is happy, he relays, and he knows his time is near its end. He just wants to hang on to say goodbye to his son and his granddaughter. Then, he's ready to board a non-stop 747 for heaven.

Did you know that there are forty-eight 2-foot by 4-foot ceiling tiles in this room? That's right, forty-eight. And you can see a few sprinkler heads stickin out through some of those ceiling tiles, including one that's right over my bed. I sure as chicken shit hope they don't have any fires while I'm here, cuz I don't feel much like takin a shower just yet. My room has eight windows in it, two of which don't have screens. I can do without the walls. Puke-yellow over cinder block doesn't do much for me. Definitely not somethin I'd have in my room back home. I share that room with my two older brothers and I know they wouldn't go for that color neither. My mom should be here soon. The nurses said she almost had a heart attack when she first saw me yesterday. I was still out cold so I didn't catch any of it. They said she busted out cryin all over my bed. And that was odd. Real odd. Tears don't come easy for my mom. She's a good lady; and she's strong, real strong inside.

Kinda the opposite of my dad. He's been dead for three years now. Part of me wants to miss him, but part of me don't. But still, with all this time on my tied-up hands, I can't control my thoughts, and lots of those thoughts send me bee-lining towards my father. I never cried at his funeral. I was proud of that at the time, but I'm not any more. I can see his grave stone. Even from here, I see it plain as day. It's carved into some unerasable part of my memory.

John Francis Foley
Born: December 15, 1928
Died: July 11, 1972
Loving Father and Husband

There. Now, you can see it too. My dad's marker is flat, barely a step above a pauper's stone. Mom drives me and my brothers and sisters out to the cemetery every Father's Day. The last time I saw Dad's stone, chunks of grass crept far across its edges. What was once a perfect "24 by 12" rectangle had become egg-shaped by those creeping blades of grass. I thought about tearin the grass from the edges but didn't. I just looked at Mom's face. It was as lifeless as Dad's stone. My little sister, Donna, started cryin. Mom pulled her in for a hug. Donna wrapped her skinny arms around Mom's waist and buried her round face in Mom's chest. I wanted out of there. I was tired of lookin at that stone. I saw enough of it already in my dreams. So I looked up into the bird-less, blue-white sky and found the sun. I opened my eyes wide, and let the sun's sniping rays do their best. I counted to five, slowly; but that wasn't good enough. I could still see. So I opened my eyes wider and counted--even slower--to ten. Then I closed my eyes and watched the sun dancing a jig inside my lids. When I opened my eyes and again looked at my father's grave stone, it was gone. Snap! Just like that. In its place was a red, glowin ball of fire.

Popp's Tavern

My Mom's hands are on my back. She never wakes me with a violent shake. She always massages the muscles on my rail-thin frame for minutes at a time before sayin a single word. I am half-asleep but somewhere in my dreams I feel my mother's warm hands caressing the wee muscles about my shoulders, my spine, my lower back.

She starts her song. It's always the same morning song. She sings it slowly and softly, each word rolling from her red lips,

"Sweet dreams are ending, the time is here,
Part your wings Angels, and give me my dear.
He's the one I love, yes, indeed, it is he,
So please hand him over, so he can go pee."

I am awake now. I roll over and smile at my mom. She's sittin on the edge of my bed. She smiles back and plants a kiss on my cheek.

"You gotta get moving, Dennis." Her smile disappears as she nods her head towards the kitchen. "He's waiting on you. I let you sleep in a little longer this morning."

"What time is it, Ma?"

"'Bout twenty past Eleven."

"Jeepers, Ma," I screech as I jump from my bed. I look over at the bunk beds next to the closet. My older brothers, Johnny and Tim, are still both asleep, with Johnny on the top bunk and Tim on the bottom. I run to the dresser, toss on some pants and a T-shirt, and slide into my low-cut Cons. I sprint out the door and into the kitchen, where I apply the brakes. My father is waiting for me, standing tall and lean like an arrow.

"C'mon," my father barks. "Let's go." He sticks a lit cigarette between his lips and walks out the back door.

"Sorry Dad." He says nothing. We walk across the porch painted 100 layers of gray with time and start down the stairs. "One sec, Dad." I jog back to the porch, grab my baseball and my brother Tim's mitt. My father glares at me. I follow him as he moves uneasily down the remaining steps.

We have a two-and-a-half block walk to Popp's Tavern. It's at 80th and Racine. We start slowly down Throop Street. I toss the ball up into the air as we walk, catching it each time with my brother's mitt. Sometimes, I throw the ball so high, I wonder if the burning sun might open its mouth and swallow the ball whole. It never does. As we walk, bungalows with stained-glass windows line both sides of the street like tiny pawns in a chess match. My own apartment is a three-flat. We pass a couple of those. In my neighborhood, each block has at least two three-flats on it. And most blocks have some six-flats and eight-flats too. We don't own our apartment. We rent the second floor unit. My dad likes second floor units. He don't care much for first floor flats. "Too many people can get atcha from the first floor." He cares even less for third floor units. "I'll be damned if I'm gonna carry all this crap up all them stairs." So, whenever we move, which is often, my father makes certain we're always sandwiched between two other families.

Fred Popp opens the door to his tavern at 11:00 am on Saturdays. My dad likes to be there as it opens. We're usually there, too. I'm normally up at 7:30 a.m. on Saturday mornings so I can watch my favorite cartoons before I leave for the tavern with my dad. Last night, though, I stayed up late with Johnny and Tim and watched *Mr. Smith Goes To Washington*, with Jimmy Stewart. What a movie! That's why I'm so late gettin started today. I know Dad's a little sore at me but he'll get over it, as soon as he has a beer in his hand.

We pass St. Sabina's on our walk. That's where I go to school. I'm in the first grade and Sister Conleth is my teacher. She's pretty nice, for a nun. She's young and she doesn't beat your hands up with the ruler like the older nuns always do. I like St. Sabina's. A lot. I have lots of friends there. Whole bunches of 'em. Last year, most of my school friends were white. Now, almost all of my school friends are black. And that's just fine with me. Right next to the school is the church, itself, and it's huge. It reaches way up into the sky and is made of creamy-colored bricks, kinda like the cone part of an ice-cream cone. Blue stained-glass windows stare at you from all over the church. My mom loves those windows. She can't walk past the church without starin at 'em. She says they're "watch-ful eyes that canvass the community." I don't quite get what that means, but I sure like the way it sounds.

When we make it to 79th Street, my father stops and lights another cigarette. Clouds of smoke swirl past his blond head and float away like lost dreams. We only have one more block to go. He moves even slower now. He beat polio as a kid, only his pencil-thin legs don't work so good any more. He's 36-years-old but I betcha I could beat him in a race.

The front door's open when we get to Popp's Tavern and the Hamm's sign above the door is swingin with the wind. My father takes his place at his stool. That's right, "his" stool. He's a regular at Popp's and all the regulars mark their stools. Mom says Dad and the other regulars are like dogs that way. I jump up on the stool beside my dad and look around. Mr. Dunleavy, Mr. O'Brien and Mr. Sheehy are already in the bar. They give my dad a wave. He waves back. None of them brought their kids today. When they do, we kids usually get into some good wrestling matches. None of us kids mind rollin around the bar floor in the beer puddles and dirt. The bar men love it. It's like they're bettin on the winner. I look around some more. Mr. Lassandrello isn't here. Good. No problems today.

Fred Popp sets a bottle of Old Style, an empty 8-ounce shorty glass, and a shot of whiskey in front of my dad. It's V.O. whiskey. I know my letters from school and that's the kinda whiskey my dad likes.

"Thanks, Fred." My father downs the shot. He pours his beer into the shorty and looks at me. I smile a stupid smile and twist back and forth on my stool. "Hey Fred, you forgot the kid." My father's no longer mad at me.

"Right," Mr. Popp says. He grabs a small bottle of Pepsi from the cooler, cracks off the cap and sets it in front of me. Mr. Popp places both hands on the bar top and stoops down to my eye level. "How's young Master Dennis doing today, Sir?" he says in a Fancy-Dan kinda voice. My dad chuckles lightly and finishes his shorty. Mr. Popp watches my dad fill his glass with golden fluid. "Can I do it to 'im, Jack?" My dad slurps more from the shorty. "Can I?" Mr. Popp again asks. My father nods his head. Mr. Popp stands straight up, a wide smile on his face. He's tall and skinny and the white apron he's wearin over his white shirt matches the white of his teeth and makes him look like a huge glow-in-the-dark toy. I know what's comin. We play this game every Saturday. Sometimes, Mr. Popp asks for my dad's permission and sometimes he don't. Mr. Popp digs his right index-finger into his right eye and plucks it from its socket. He sets the glass eye on the bar top next to me. "Don't go getting into any trouble now, Master Dennis. I'll be watching you." I can stare at that fake eyeball all day long. I know it isn't real. What I can't do, though, is look at the empty eye socket on Mr. Popp's face. I looked at it once, just once. It was red and raw and kinda dark, like someone stuffed some half-cooked hamburger meat in there. I threw-up when I looked that time, to the delight of my dad and the other bar men. I learned to wait until Mr. Popp had enough time to slip the black patch over his eye. I usually count to 25. Sometimes my dad whispers, "He put the patch on." Today, I count to 25 and when I look up, Mr. Popp is standing in front of Mr. Dunleavy and the patch is in place.

"The Pirate." That's what my mom calls Mr. Popp. She doesn't care much for him. "The Pirate steals the food from the mouths of the young," she says, "and turns it into whiskey for their fathers to drink and forget." I've been coming to Popp's Tavern with my dad for about a year now. I know why I'm here. I'm young but I'm not as dumb as you might think. Actually, my mom told me why I hafta go with my dad. "Just stay with him, be with him, and that way he won't forget any of us." I'm a permanent reminder for my dad that he has a wife and six kids who need things, like food, at home. I am here to remind him that he better have some money in his pocket when we leave Mr. Popp.

Whenever Mom asks me what goes on at Popp's, I always lie. "Nothin," I tell her and then keep on lyin by tellin her that I don't like the place much at all. Truth is, those are major lies cuz I like everything about Popp's Tavern.

Mr. Popp's place always smells like stale beer no matter how many times he drags his old, gray-haired mop across the wooden floor. I love that smell. The mirror behind the bar goes on forever. Wherever I'm at in the bar, I can always find my freckled face starin back at me. I like to watch smoke fly outta the mouths of the drinking men and climb to the tin ceiling where it hangs like a bunch of dirty clouds. You should see Mr. Popp clean the shorty glasses and shot glasses. He runs hot water through 'em, shoves a towel inside 'em and smushes the towel around 'til the glasses are both dry and clean. It only takes Mr. Popp five seconds to clean and dry a glass. I timed him before. Once the glasses are clean, Mr. Popp sets 'em back on the bar top where they stand in line and wait their turn to be used again.

Now I know I'm a munchkin but still I feel like one of the guys when I'm at Popp's. The other men always make a point to say hello to me, pinch my cheek, pat me on the back, or say somethin about my flaming hair. My dad lets me drink Pepsi 'til my belly's set to burst, I get to play the bowling ball machine, and I get to see a few good fights, too. The best was when Mr. Sheehy and Mr. Everett got into it. Mr. Everett's a little guy with a pointy, red beard. He looks like the Lucky

Charms leprechaun. And Mr. Sheehy's as big as John Wayne. Anyway, Mr. Sheehy was poundin the stuffins outta Mr. Everett. He knocked him to the floor at least three times. Mr. Everett wouldn't quit, though. He kept wipin the blood from his mouth and comin back for more. When he was on the ground the last time, Mr. Sheehy said, in his thick brogue, "Listen you little squirt, just stay down there like the dog ya are." The bar men all laughed. Mr. Sheehy took his eyes offa Mr. Everett and laughed with all the others. That was a big mistake. From his knees, Mr. Everett slammed his fist into Mr. Sheehy's crotch. "Ooohh," all the bar men said at the same time. Goliath grabbed his marbles and fell with a thud to the floor. He stayed there a good, long while, fixing himself in all the right places. An hour later, the two men were drinking together, and Mr. Sheehy even thanked Mr. Everett for sockin him in the spot. He said, "Actually, Everett, it should be me Missus who should be thankin ya. You've found an effective means of birth control for the Irish." I didn't quite know what that meant either. But I do know that enemies don't stay enemies very long at Popp's.

Mostly, though, I like being at Popp's 'cuz I get to be with my dad, all by myself. Most times he doesn't say much to me, but sometimes he answers my questions. He talks to me about the Cubs a bunch. He likes all the Chicago teams but the Cubs are definitely his favorite. He's not much help when I hit him with my homework questions though. "Ask your mother," is what he says then. Either way, I really don't care. I just wanna be with him. I like watching my dad wipe the beer foam from his mouth after taking a long gulp from his shorty. He likes to shoot cigarette smoke at the ceiling, too. Sometimes, when he knows I'm watchin, he'll blow little chunks of smoke from his mouth that form perfect tiny rings that could fit around your finger. The rings grow and grow as they rise and they always fall apart just before they get a chance to bang into the ceiling. My mother doesn't like what my father does with his cigarette ashes, though. Ashtrays are everywhere at Popp's but my father has no use for 'em. When he drinks, he sits with his back smushed into the back support and his right leg crossed over his left. He always flicks his ashes into the cuff of his right pant leg and he always wears cuffed pants. My mom's the one who gets stuck cleanin those cuffed pants.

My older brothers, John and Tim, used to come with my dad to the tavern but they don't come anymore. I don't know why. Whenever I ask them why, they never answer. They're teenagers now and they don't seem to care much about Dad anymore. They're missin out on a lot. I think ya get kinda stupid when you become a teenager. I feel sorry for my three sisters. They never get to come to Popp's. My Mom would never let 'em. "A tavern is no place for a little lady," Mom says. They're missin out, too. I sometimes tell my sister Sharon what happens at Popp's and she can't believe it. She gets all filled up with, "He did what? Who punched who?"and "Who fell offa the stool?" You know how girls can get. Sometimes I even get to come with my dad on Wednesdays and Fridays. Those are his three biggest days, but Saturday is definitely the biggest.

My father drinks lotsa shots and beers as the day passes. He smokes and joins in manly chit-chat, too. The day goes along smoothly, mostly cuz Mr. Lassandrello didn't show up. This Saturday ends like most other Saturdays. At 5:00, Mr. Popp tells us to go home. He knows our schedule.

"I'll be taking me eye back now, Master Dennis," Mr. Popp says. "You've been a fine wee lad, today. Now, get goin' before the real Master throws your supper out the window." Mr. Popp grabs his eye from the bar top as my dad and I head out the door. I don't watch him stuff it back in place. Mr. Popp's right. It is indeed supper-time. Ah yes, Saturday, supper-time. Stew night. I'm ready for it. I flip the ball into the sky over and over again as we walk home, catching it each time. Sometimes I don't get to toss the ball on the walk home, but my dad doesn't need to lean on me tonight.

Batman

It was a steamy summer night. The front windows of the apartment were open wide, and there were no screens. Mom was at the store and we kids were home with Dad, all of us packed like rats on the floor in front of the TV, gettin ready for the start of the Ed Sullivan show. A fan hummed on low speed in the corner. Dad lounged on the couch, an Old Style in his hand. His view of the tube was blocked. He let us know.

"C'mon already," he yelped. "Move your big skulls outta the way. I can't see a damn thing." Johnny and Tim worked their way back towards the couch, dragging their getting-hairier-by-the-day bodies across the hardwood floor. Sharon and Jackie boarded the two living room chairs like civilized ladies, and Donna and I pushed ourselves onto the floor like crawling army men. We heard no further complaints so Dad's view musta been just fine. Watching the Ed Sullivan Show was a must every Sunday night. It was one of the few things we did as a family. There was music for the young, comedians for the old, and variety acts for all. I liked to imitate Mr. Sullivan and did so during most every commercial break, repeating his line, "Tonight, we have a really great sh-h-h-how," bringing smiles to everyone's faces. But on this night, there would be no Sullivan Show. Not for us anyway. Something else was preparing to pay us a visit, and that something flew right in one of the front windows and smashed directly into the TV screen. It lay there on the floor, just one foot away from my gazing-at-Ed-Sullivan face. My eyes turned down upon this black winged creature. It was stunned from the blow and beat it's wings twice, quite slowly, trying to regain its balance. I tried to close my eyes but couldn't. I was frozen.

"A ba-a-a-t," Donna screeched. She jumped to her feet and catapulted herself onto Dad's lap. Footsteps scampered behind me. Everyone now was back with my father on the couch. Everyone except me. I was still frozen.

"Okay, Sport, c'mon back here," Dad whispered, hoping a soft voice wouldn't spook the bat. I tried to move but couldn't. It was as if my legs were shackled tight to the floor. Mr. Sullivan's voice rang loud and clear. The noisy Sullivan crowd chuckled.

"C'mon Sport," Dad said. His voice was louder this time. I still couldn't move. "Now!" The bat was standing on his feet, flexing his wings. He was no longer stunned. He was very much alive. His dull eyes clung to his face like a pair of tarred BB's, and his tiny black ears stood alert atop his furry head. He turned his head from side to side, sizing up the situation. He looked very much like a tiny rat with wings, minus the tail. My eyes finally closed. I tucked my head into my arms.

"He's gonna bite him, Daddy," Donna cried. My dad set his beer down on the wooden floor with a bang. I opened my eyes and just in time. Dad jumped from the couch and dove for the bat, his long arms and spindly fingers outstretched. The bat screeched and flew up into the ceiling. The Sullivan audience laughed. Suddenly, my shackles shook loose. I jumped to my feet and ran for the couch. Dad scraped himself off the floor. He turned and looked at us, a thin smile on his face. He broke out into soft laughter. The looks of doom fell from our faces and we too fell apart laughing. The Sullivan audience once again joined us. The bat hovered briefly near the ceiling and then took off down the shotgun hallway into the kitchen.

Dad turned towards the kitchen. "C'mon. We gotta get him outta there and back out here, out the window." We followed Dad.

"But he might bite us Daddy," Donna said.

"Yah, and then you'll be a little vampire," Johnny said.

"Daddy, make 'im stop," Donna cried.

"Knock if off," Dad barked. My brother did as ordered.

As we crept towards the kitchen, a band played a song on the Sullivan show and the screams of the crowd pushed us forward. Once in the kitchen, we flocked around the kitchen table and ran our eyes all over the ceiling, walls, and floor, but we didn't see that bat anywhere. All I saw were stains on the wooden floor and chips of light blue paint breaking free of the walls. Dad grabbed a fly swatter that was hanging off a nail by the back door and readied it for action in his left hand.

"I'm scared, Daddy." It was Donna again.

"Then go in the front room, Sweetie."

"Ok, Daddy."

"You'll be all alone in there my little vampire," Johnny said, doing his best Bela Lugosi, "and then he'll come to suck your blood."

"I'll stay here instead, Daddy." Donna huddled behind Tim and wrapped her tiny arms around his solid waist. Tim reached back with his right hand and rested it on her shoulder. The bat that none of us could see suddenly darted about the kitchen. He had been lying low, pressed flat like a leaf atop the fridge. He came right at my dad and Dad swung the fly swatter twice at him but missed. The bat then darted back to the front room. We raced back there, following our father, our feet pounding the floor. Once in the front room, Dad screeched to a halt. The rest of us didn't. Our eyes were fixed on the bat. Bing, Bang, Bammo. Johnny smashed into Dad, and Tim tackled Johnny, and the rest of us plowed into the three of them. A pile of fair skin, freckles, and arms and legs of all sizes and shapes laid atop the front room floor. The Sullivan audience rang loud with laughter. We quickly scraped ourselves off the floor and saw the bat hovering in a corner away from the front window. His black body seemed even blacker against the whitewashed walls.

"Tim, go grab a blanket offa your bed," Dad ordered. Tim moved to action. "And close the hallway door when you come back." Dad didn't take his eyes off the flying rat.

"Johnny, you go by the light switch." He moved there. The rest of us huddled around Dad. "When I say so, I want ya to turn the switch off. Then wait for me to say, 'Now,' and then I want ya to flick the switch on and off real fast. Understand?"

"Gottit," Johnny said. With his eyes still on the bat, Dad reached over and turned off Mr. Sullivan's show. Silence came to the room, but from that silence came the wings of the bat beating wildly to stay afloat. And the more I listened, the more I thought the wings were a soothing sound--almost like the purr of a cat.

Tim came back with the blanket and gave it to my dad. "The hallway door's closed," he said.

"Good." Dad opened the blanket slowly until it draped in front of him. "All right, the rest of you stand over by the door. Move nice and slow now." Dad's voice was barely a step above a whisper. We slid our feet over to the door.

"Okay, Johnny, kill the light." Darkness fell upon the room. I couldn't see anything for several seconds, but I heard the slow movement of my father's feet tip-toeing across the floor. Then tiny specs of light crawled out from the kitchen and slid under the hallway door. My father's shape glided towards the corner where the bat was.

"Now," Dad said. Johnny switched the light on and off as fast as he could. In what seemed like freeze-frame, slow motion, Dad swung the blanket up and tossed it at the bat. Then the bat was gone and the blanket clumped to the floor. Dad's plan worked.

"Leave the light on," Dad barked. Johnny flicked the light on one last time and all of us edged toward the clump. Little puffs of blanket vibrated as the bat struggled to move.

Johnny started towards the kitchen. "I'll go get a broom to smash 'im with," he said.

"Hold on there," Dad said. "Hold on just a second." Johnny came back.

"Well, aren't you gonna kill 'im?" Johnny said.

Dad rubbed the stubby hairs on his chin. "I don't think we should." He rubbed the stubby hairs again. "He's probably got a wife and kids of his own waitin for 'im in some little bat cave somewheres." Dad bent down and balled up the blanket so the bat couldn't escape, but left enough room for him to breath. "You wouldn't wanna kill him with that being the case. Right?"

"Right, Dad," we all said, except for Johnny. He stayed silent.

"Stay here." Dad walked out the front door and raced down the steps with the bat in hand. We stuck our heads out the front windows when he appeared below. He looked up at us and pointed. "Hey, close those windows. We don't wanna go hunting again tonight." We did as asked and then pressed our noses against the window glass. Dad grabbed a corner of the blanket and snapped it open into the night. I didn't see the bat take off. I don't think anyone did except for Dad. His head jerked when the bat flew past him, before it blended in with the darkness.

After Dad came upstairs, he flicked the TV on. Mr. Sullivan stared into our faces. "I hope you've enjoyed our sh-h-h-how, and we'll see you again next week." The audience clapped. I felt like the audience was clapping for my father and I fully expected him to take a bow. The front door popped open. Mom strolled in with a single bag of groceries in her hand. She looked at the TV.

"How was the Sullivan show?" she asked.

"We didn't watch it, Hun," Dad said. Mom's eyebrows shot up.

"Oh, no. Why not?"

"We were bat hunting, Mommy," Donna said.

Mom shook her head. "Bat hunting, huh?" It was obvious she didn't believe us. She wagged her head as she strode toward the kitchen. "Now there's a popular form of family entertainment." We all looked at each other and laughed, and then Dad grabbed his beer and took a long, long gulp.

Holy Cross Hospital--Day 3

When my mom came to visit today, she spent the whole day just sittin next to me. She read the comics to me from the Sun-Times. That Beetle Bailey cracks me up. I busted a gut laughin over his antics and my body hurt like hell at first. But I'm feelin better now. The pain aint so bad.

The old-timer's still here. His family still hasn't shown up. I feel bad for him. He was awake all day wearin a I-sure-hope-they-come-soon-cuz-I-can't-last-much-longer look on his wrinkled wrinkled face. He's been strugglin with that oxygen mask. I know he hates to wear it. He keeps taking it off. And then, when the breathing gets hard on him, he slips it back on. There's no brainwaves passin between us today. I don't know why. There just aint. So I can't tell ya what he's thinkin. But still, I wonder who this old guy is. His arms were out on top of his sheets today and I saw the tattoo he has on his right forearm. I've seen some like it before on a few of the old-timers back at Popp's Tavern. It's some sort of a World War II Army insignia. I'd like to ask the old-timer about it, but I know it's tough for him to breath, let alone talk.

My step-father came with my mom today, too. He didn't stay the whole time, though. His name's John. He's a good guy. They've been married for almost two years now. Anyone who marries a lady with six kids is A-Ok in my book. My brothers and sisters are supposed to come see me tomorrow. That's only if I keep gettin stronger. That's what the nurses tell me. And I am doing better. Since I've gotten used to the pain, they took the ropes offa me. Can you spell F-r-e-e-d-o-m? It feels good to be able to move a little. But my movement is still kinda limited. I stay on my back or on my right side so as not to screw up that chest tube under my left pit. But just being able to move my arms and legs feels great.

Bobby, Hairdo, Finn and Spud called me on the telephone. Their real names are: Bobby Malloy, Harry Everest, Pat Finnegan, and Michael Flynn. They were all together at Hairdo's house when they called so they passed the phone around. The O'Grady twins, Marty and Danny, called later in the day. I told all my buddies I was doin just fine and that I might get out in about ten more days. The doctors wanna keep me for a while yet in this ICU to make sure my lung keeps gettin stronger. That's where the knife went--straight into my left lung. At first, they were worried that the knife also nicked my aorta. That's what the medicine men told me and my mom. I don't know where the aorta is exactly, but I know it's a big feeder to the heart. Since there hasn't been any leakage yet, the doctors think the knife just missed. They think I'm out of major danger. I told my buddies all that. They said they'd drink a beer for me tonight. I told 'em to have several.

The doctors won't let my buddies come visit. Only family can come to the ICU, I am told. The boys can come visit when I go to a regular room. I'm not a big fan of rules. Fact is, I'd like to see my friends. I wanna thank 'em in person. After all, they're the ones who got me to the hospital in time, the ones who saved me. If ya ask me, the hospital should let 'em in, and throw the red-carpet out for 'em to prance across like kings.

Christmas, 1965

The first time Dad got real sick was a few months before Christmas in 1965. I was still in first-grade then. Mom said he went to some place to get his stomach better. The place Dad went to was called the sanitarium. It would be his first of many, many visits. Dad still wasn't home when December stormed in. There was no tree that Christmas and since we didn't have a tree, I kinda figured there weren't gonna be any presents either. But Mom searched and found an opportunity for us kids to snag some gifts.

I stood in a long line with my brothers and sisters and hundreds of other kids that snaked through the center aisle of some auditorium in downtown Chicago. Some people just sat in the seats on either side of that aisle and stared straight ahead like they were waitin for the Sunday matinee to come on. We were all about to meet Gale Sayers and Dick Butkus, the rookie stars of the Chicago Bears. My dad was a huge Butkus fan. He loved the way he steamrolled quarterbacks and running backs. Sayers made him foam at the mouth. "Look at that guy run," he'd say whenever Sayers had the ball. And now I was about to meet these mighty Bears in the flesh.

Mom brought us to the auditorium. She tried hard to keep a smile on her face as she urged us forward from the back of the line. She was tryin to set the example. It didn't work. Every time I turned back to look at her, her lips were flat and her face blank. When she noticed my stare, she'd show me her happy teeth. None of my brothers and sisters said much as the line crept forward, cept for Donna. She kept on bouncin up and down like a pogo stick and sayin, "Raggedy Ann, Raggedy Ann." Mom told her that's what the good little girls were gettin as presents. When my turn came, I climbed up into the large lap of Dick Butkus. His legs were solid, no doubt cut from the mightiest of Oak trees. A Santa hat leaned to the side atop his head. He looked anything but ferocious. And then I saw his eyes. They weren't the killer eyes that went buggy on the football field. He had sad eyes that were connected to his I-feel-sorry-for-ya-kid look on his whole face. I knew then that somethin was wrong with me, with my family. Dick Butkus was rough and tough. He wasn't supposed to feel sorry for anyone, yet here he was sayin nice things to me, all the while starin at me with those sad eyes. After a bit, Mr. Butkus set me off his lap and handed me a toy tool box. It was painted shiny red and had a metal handle right on top. I thanked Mr. Butkus and carried the tool box to a table at the back of the auditorium where I opened it. Inside the box, there was a small wooden hammer, saw and screw driver. And then I saw the tag. I missed it at first. It was taped to the side of the toolbox. It said MERRY CHRISTMAS but there was no name in the TO and FROM sections.

I looked back at Mr. Butkus. Another kid was lookin small in his lap. The kid wore a torn sweater and had dirty pants on. I looked at my own clothes. They weren't any better. And then I saw Mr. Butkus' face. He looked at this kid the same way he looked at me. I shifted my eyes to Mr. Sayers. Though the Kansas Comet was black and Mr. Butkus was white, they were twins that day. Both wore identical sad expressions on their faces.

When we left that day for home, I didn't bring the tool box. I left it in on the table in that auditorium--on purpose. I decided that I'd rather have nothin for Christmas than to play with a tool set that would forever remind me of how others felt sorry for me. Especially, big tough Chicago Bears.

Mike, the Cat

I'm walking down 79th Street with my dad, heading for Popp's Tavern. It's about 5 minutes to 11:00, Saturday morning. We'll be there as the door opens so my dad is happy. I'm tossing a ball into the air and catchin it with my mitt. That's right, my mitt. It's a Juan Marichal special with the name scribbled right across the crease. My dad bought it for me. He has a new job at the horse racetrack. You mighta seen my dad before if you bet on the horses. He's one of them guys who stands behind the window with the jail bars across it and takes your money and bets. Mom says it's the best job Dad ever had. "The pay is good," she tells me. "We might be able to get our own house before long." I'm glad my dad has his new job. I like my new mitt.

When we get to Popp's, we slip onto our stools. Mr. Roche and Mr. Flannery are just a few seats away. They're passing around one of those bar napkins with the cheesy jokes and squawking like crows. Mr. Popp sets a beer and shot in front of my dad and snaps the cap off of a Pepsi for me.

Mr. Roche is talking loud and I'm wondering if he's drunk already. But how can a guy be drunk already, if Mr. Popp just opened his front door?

"You gonna go over there today?" Mr. Roche says.

"Wouldn't miss it for the world," Mr. Flannery says. I turn on my stool and face Mr. Flannery. I want to know what he's talking about.

"What time you plan on goin?"

Before Mr. Flannery can answer, from three stools away Mr. D'Amico jumps in. "I heard they aint comin today. I heard they're comin tomorrow."

"No they're not, numb nuts," says Mr. Roche. "They're movin in today." I spin away on my chair for a second. Numb nuts. Those words always crack me up. I don't want Mr. Roche or Mr. Flannery or Mr. D'Amico to see me laughin.

"Who told ya that?" says Mr. Flannery.

I am done laughing now so I spin back around. Mr. Roche downs his shot and says, "The realtor, Bernie Ryan, told me so." A little bit of whiskey dribble slides down towards his chin. He erases it with his shirt sleeve.

"The realtor?" Mr. Flannery turns his eyes into slits and aims them at Roche. "You still talkin to him? You oughta break his fuckin nose."

"Or slit his throat," Mr. D'Amico adds.

"Ya hear dat?" Mr. Roche says with a laugh. "Dom wants to slit his throat." He wags his head and takes a swig of beer. "What's with Dagos and wantin to slit everyone's throats all the time? I mean, every Dago I ever met keeps a little black book filled with the names of everyone who's got a throat slittin coming to 'em."

Mr. D'Amico laughs. He is a small, bald man with fuzzy black eyebrows, and when he laughs those eyebrows look like caterpillars dancin on his forehead. He raises his glass but stops before he takes a drink. His eyes are resting on my father. "How 'bout you, Jack? You gonna bring some lemonade and cookies over to your new neighbors today?"

My dad shifts his eyes towards Mr. D'Amico but then slowly turns back. He grabs his pack of cigarettes and picks at the plastic wrap.

Mr. D'Amico takes a big swig of beer. "So did you do it, Jack?"

There are eleven men in the bar now and they all have their eyes set on my dad.

"Do what?" my dad says.

Mr. D'Amico smiles. "C'mon, Jack. The cat. Mrs. O'Neil's cat. Was it you?"

From the far end of the bar, Mr. Sheehy yells out, "What cat? What the hell ya talkin about?"

"Are you kiddin me," Mr. D'Amico says. "You haven't heard this shit?"

"Nope."

Mr. D'Amico starts in again. "Okay, so this is how it goes. When word spread that the O'Neil's sold their home to that shine family, their big Persian cat, Mike—"

"Yah, I know that cat," says Mr. Sheehy. "Big and fat."

"Damn right he's big and fat," says Mr. D'Amico. "He's also fathered more offspring that a carload of horny Mormons. Anyway, after word spread that the O'Neils sold to shines, old Mike was found hanging from a light post out in front of the O'Neils' bungalow."

Mr. Sheehy climbs off his stool as if he was on a horse and walks down towards Mr. D'Amico. So does Mr. Keane. Mr. D'Amico looks around at all the eyes on him. He's a good storyteller. I could listen to him all day.

"You shoulda seen it. His big, fat body was stiff as hell and his tiny red tongue fell outta his mouth. Sorta like this." Mr. D'Amico tilts his head to the side and drops his tongue out of his mouth. A few guys laugh. "Anyways, Mr. O'Neil cut Mike down from the light post, and Mrs. O'Neil nearly had a heart attack when she found out what happened."

"No shit. I didn't hear about any of this," says Mr. Sheehy.

"But that aint the end of it," says Mr. D'Amico. "See, Mrs. O'Neil's all sad and crying. I mean, you know they aint got any kids or nothin and Mike was kinda like a kid to them, so she tells her husband to go dig a little hole in the back yard, and like the royal kiss ass that he is, he does just what his queen tells him to do. So he wraps Mike up in a burlap sack and buries 'im in the backyard. He even puts a little popsicle stick cross on top of him in the dirt." Mr. D'Amico stops to take a slug of beer. Then he dabs at his eyes and laughs. "Very touching stuff, ya know. Enough to make a grown man want to cry."

Mr. Popp is not pouring any shots or beers for anyone in the bar. All eleven men in the bar are listening to Mr. D'Amico. Even Mr. Popp is glued in to Mr. D'Amico. His hands are stapled to the bar counter, his patch eye staring at Mr. D'Amico. All of the men have matching thin smiles on their faces.

"Oh go on already," Mr. Flannery says and laughs. "Keep tellin it."

Mr. D'Amico is glad to continue. "Okay, so the very next day, Mrs. O'Neil does actually have a heart attack."

"No shit?" says Mr. Sheehy.

"She's okay though. She's still kickin. See, she went out to the backyard to say a few prayers over Mike's grave and--" Mr. D'Amico starts to laugh. He can't stop himself. He takes a couple of big breaths, snorting like a pig, and then one big slug of beer.

"What?" says Mr. Sheehy. "C'mon already. Spit it out."

"Okay, okay" Mr. D'Amico sets his beer down. "So the popsicle stick's gone and the grave's all dug up. Mrs. O'Neil's in a panic. She's searchin around the yard and there's no Mike anywhere. So she looks under the porch and then beside the garage and still no Mike. Then she runs out into the front yard and lo and behold, there's Mike, strung up on that same lightpost. Again."

"You shittin me?"

"Nope. So right then and there Mrs. O'Neil drops to the ground. Mr. O runs out to help his wife and sees Mike twistin in the wind. He runs in and calls the ambulance and then comes back out and while he's waitin, he starts screamin. And I mean screamin for the whole neighborhood to hear. 'FUCKERS. YOU'RE ALL FUCKERS, YOU HEAR ME?' So he takes off with his wife in the ambulance and Mike's still there on the post. Mr. O musta called the cops from the hospital cuz they came out later and cut old Mike down.

Mr. Sheehy raises his glass of beer. “Join me, lads. Join me please.” All the bar men, including my father, raise their glasses. “To Mike. Let’s drink to Mike, the horniest cat known to man.” Glasses are clanked together like bells in a church and the barmen laugh. When the laughter is over, Mr. D’Amico again stares at my father.

“Well Jack,” Mr. D’Amico says, “the question still stands. Did you do it?”

My dad stabs his cigarette into the leather sole of his shoe, drops the butt to the wooden floor. His eyes fall upon me. He then turns his stool towards Mr. D’Amico.

“Which time?” my dad says.

Popp’s Tavern explodes with laughter.

Willie and Winston

The mouse trap screamed. I looked across the kitchen table at my friend, Willie. His eyes were spread wide, starin at me. His brother, Winston, grabbed my arm.

"You hear dat?" Winston said.

My mother stood just a few feet from us, cooking our lunch at the stove, a frilly, blue apron that matched the color of the kitchen walls bow-tied 'round her waist. Grilled cheese sandwiches hissed in the butter.

I said nothin. We all knew the sound. Willie and Winston lived just down the street with their mom and gramma and they sure as heck had mice, just as we had mice. I jumped from my chair and ran to the fridge, my glass of pop in hand. On the floor, in the one-foot space between the fridge and the big window that looked out over the back porch and yard, I found the mousetrap.

I bent over to take a look and Winston bumped into me. A single ice-cube spilled out of my glass and landed directly on the mouse's head. It did no further damage. The mouse was already dead. I pushed the cube away and took a closer look.

"Lemme see, lemme see," Winston said. This mouse would never sing or dance or play catch again. The bar came right down across his neck. I'd seen other mice in traps before, squirming and squeaking. Not this one. His neck was crushed, forcing his mouth to open wide. He displayed the tiniest of teeth.

Willie and Winston were breathing hard over my shoulder. I grabbed the mouse and trap and stood up, making certain I didn't touch his furry black body. I pulled him to my chest and cradled him like a show and tell piece. Willie and Winston both moved in for a closer look. Winston shot his right hand at the mouse and touched his fur with his brown finger.

"Ick," Willie said.

"Get rid of that thing and wipe your filthy mitts," Mom said. "The sandwiches are almost ready."

"But don't ya wanna see 'im, ma?"

"Does a bear poop in a toilet?" That was Mom for ya. She liked to answer a question with another question that provided the obvious answer. Willie set both of his hands on the back screen door and pushed it open. His arms and hands were darker than his brother's. They were the color of the mouse. Winston grabbed a pack of matches from the window sill as he walked out the door onto the back porch.

"Lemme see, lemme see," Winston said again. I liked being in control. Again I held the mouse at waist level. Willie and Winston moved closer. Winston dropped to his knees to get a better look. His light gray shorts seemed to melt into the battleship-gray porch floor. His eyes were at the same level as the dead mouse.

"See the blood?" Winston said, pointing at my mouse. I missed that. I raised the mouse to my own eye level. Then I saw it. Winston was right. One lonely speck of blood rested on the corner of the trap. It was the size of half a tear drop.

"C'mon," I said, "let's bury it." Willie and I moved towards the stairs.

"No," Winston shouted.

I turned back. Willie's eyes were fixed on his younger brother.

"Let's burn it."

"What?" Willie and I both said.

"Burn him," Winston said, his face filled with teeth. "I done it befo' to an old squirrel I found squished in the alley." Winston stopped for a second to stick his finger in his ear. He twisted it back and forth and then pulled it out. "At first, he started to burn real slow. Den, his bushy tail got to goin fast and he was a complete scorcher in no time flat."

"You crazy," Willie said.

I shook my head and aimed a mean stare at Winston.

"We aint gonna burn him. He's my mouse so we'll—"

"Why's he yo' mouse?" Winston said.

"Cuz he was in my house."

Winston stapled his hands to his hips. "Well, he coulda been in my house befo' and then followed me here to visit. So, he might just as much be my mouse as he is yo' mouse."

"No he aint," I said through tight lips. I pushed my face right up to Winston's and hawked my eyes. Only a few inches separated us. "He died in my house so he's my mouse." I shoved Winston back. "We'll dig a little hole and bury him."

"Time to eat boys," Mom yelled through the kitchen window.

I set the mouse on the porch banister. "Let's leave him here for now." His furry, black body looked cozy atop the gray-everywhere banister. I kept my eyes on Winston. I knew he wanted that mouse bad. I made him go through the back door before me. "We'll get him later," I said. Winston didn't look too happy.

We plopped ourselves in the kitchen chairs and feasted on my mom's food. Grilled cheese, pickles and applesauce. Me and my friends were all smilin again. I liked it better this way. But still, who ever heard of burnin a mouse, or any dead animal? That's sick. We passed around the glass of Pepsi, all of our lips not mindin that the others' lips touched the glass.

The back door flew open. My father stood there, the dead mouse layin in the palm of his hand--looking very small and lost. Dad was back from the sanitarium but he was trying to catch up on the time he lost at Popp's Tavern by goin even more now.

"Who the hell left this on the porch?" The smell of Mr. Popp's place flew offa his lips. He raised the mouse and trap in the air like the guys do at weddings, when they're makin a toast. "We look like a bunch of hillbillies with dead mice layin all over."

"Mind your words, Jack," Mom said. My father glared at my mother. My mother glared right back.

"Who?" Dad said.

"I-I-I did, Dad." I had to squeeze each word out. Willie and Winston stared at my father, their eyes wide and unblinking. My father stared back.

"Whatcha lookin' at?" my father said, pointing his bony, right index finger at Willie. Willie's eyes fell to his plate. Winston's eyes did the same. My dad looked at my mother. "I told you before about these two," he barked. Again he pointed. This time his index finger wavered like a sword back and forth from Willie to Winston. "I don't want these God-damn nig—"

"Jack!" my mother screamed. My father stopped talking.

"What?" he snarled.

"I'll give you 'What'." She knotted her hands across her chest. Her face was pinched. "Go to bed and sleep it off." Lines raced across my mother's face and her teeth were showing, like a growling dog. "We don't need to hear your crap."

Willie and Winston kept on starin holes into their plates. My father kicked open the back screen door and, before the door had a chance to close, tossed my mouse out onto the porch. I watched him somersault and turn and twist in the air before he finally clanked off the porch floor. My father then backed away, circling his way through the kitchen like a boxer in the ring. I watched him until he finally made it to his room, where he slammed the door shut.

I looked at Willie and Winston. Their eyes hadn't moved yet. I wanted to say something to make everyone feel better. My mom did, instead.

"Eat up and share your pop, boys." She took off her apron, balled it up and tossed it atop the fridge. "And be glad that you're drinking pop, too, instead of whiskey like Mr. Foley." Willie and Winston lifted their eyes from their plates. My mother was smiling. I smiled too. "That's right boys. And when you get to be an old geezer like my husband, don't go 'round drinking whiskey all the time." My mother laughed. "Mr. Foley's a fine example of how whiskey melts the brain." We all laughed. My mother took a seat at the table and watched us eat. I was glad she was on our side. We ate our food and drank the pop, and all of us were glad that it was pop we were drinkin and not whiskey. We all knew my mother was full of wisdom. When we finished, we stuck our plates in the sink.

"See ya, Ma," I said. "We'll be in the alley."

"Thanks, Mrs. Foley," Willie said.

"Me too, Mrs. Foley," hollered Winston. My mother patted both of my friends upon their heads.

"You're both very welcome."

We buried the mouse and Winston didn't seem to mind much. Only thing was, I couldn't stop thinkin that Winston was gonna dig the mouse up later and burn him. With the mouse planted, we played with Winston's Superball in the alley. You had to be a good shot to play with a Superball in the alley. There wasn't much room. Not only did you hafta smack the ball off the cement and make it sail high into the sky, but you hadta make sure it landed on the cement again, avoiding the garages and garbage cans that lined both sides of the alley.

"My turn," Willie said.

"No it aint. It's mines," Winston said.

"It's Willie's turn," I said. I liked being the judge.

Willie tossed a good toss. The striped ball bounced off the concrete, sailed about forty feet into the sky and landed about twenty feet from us. We chased it down.

"Dat aint nuthin," Winston bragged. He showed us his teeth and twisted the ball around with his fingers. "Watch dis." Winston lifted his left foot high into the sky, like Giants pitcher Juan Marichal, brang that foot down and whipped the ball into the cement. The ball exploded into the sky. I lost it in the sun. Then I saw it again—rising, rising, rising, and then falling, falling, falling. "Here it come," Winston yelled. As the ball neared the ground, Winston shot his right hand out and snatched the ball like it was the easiest thing in the world to do. Only I knew it wasn't.

"Dang," I said. Winston was the best. And Willie and I knew it.

"Fergie Jenkins, man," Winston said. "Fergie Jenkins. That's who I'm gonna pitch like when I'm growed up. I'm pitchin fo' the Cubs too." We all loved Fergie. He was the best pitcher on the Cubs. We shoulda been White Sox fans since we lived on the Southside, but all three of us were Cubs fans. Mostly cuz of Fergie and cuz of Ernie Banks, the Cubs home-run king.

Willie and Winston's gramma came down the alley. She didn't get too close but I still knew it was her. She had that same ol' spotted-red bandana tied over her hair like Aunt Jemima on the pancake box, and she had a tiny piece of a cigarette glowin between her lips. She probably just found that cigarette butt on the ground. I never saw that lady with a full cig. She had a way of findin the little half-smoked ones on the ground and savin 'em like pennies for when she needed 'em.

"C'mon home boys," she hollered.

When Willie and Winston left, I went back to my apartment. Dad's door was still closed but Mom was gone. I figured she went to the store. Sharon and Donna were in the front room watchin somethin on the TV. But I wasn't in the mood for TV. I grabbed a 100-piece puzzle and started snappin it together on the kitchen table. I was kinda thirsty, too. But there wasn't any more pop in the fridge so I grabbed a glass of water. I don't know how long I was workin on the puzzle but it musta been a while. It was more than half done. Most of Soldier Field--where the Bears play--was laid out flat on the kitchen table, starin me square in the face. My dad was awake now, only I didn't know it.

As I pieced in part of a fluffy white cloud floating above Soldier Field, I felt a tremendous tear at my hair. My head was being yanked backwards. I almost fell outta my chair. Instead, the chair teetered on its hind legs like a dog beggin for a treat. My father leaned over me. He was standing directly behind me, peering down. His face was red, his forehead crinkled. His lips were twisted open and I could see his snarling teeth pressed tightly together.

"Don't ever bring those little niggers 'round here again. Ever." He shook my head back and forth and then stopped. "You gottit?"

I said nothin. I could really smell the whiskey on him. The stink was wrapped around each one of his growling teeth. I just looked at him, wondering what to do or say. He pushed his face even closer and yanked my head again. "You gottit?" he screamed, louder than before.

"Yah, Dad," I whispered. "I got it." He let go of my hair and my chair came back to the ground. Dad then poured a glass of milk for himself and after he downed it, he walked slowly back to his bedroom. He closed the door, but there was no slam this time.

The word "nigger" was almost never said in our apartment, least not when Mom was around. I could count its usage on one hand. When one of my older brothers used the word, Mom always treated the situation the same. She'd grab em round their collar and threaten, "You say that word one more time, just one more time, and you'll be eatin' a bar of soap for dinner." Then she'd shake 'em like they were boneless dolls. I never said the word. Never. Truth be told, I didn't really know what the word meant. I know that might sound stupid, but it's the truth. I knew it was a bad word, though. As bad as Mother-Fucker, even. I said that word once. I didn't know what that word meant either but I knew it was bad. I heard Johnny call one of his friends a Mother-Fucker once when he was mad. So when I got mad at Tim one day, I called him a Mother-Fucker. My mom was in the same room. She scrubbed my tongue with Dial soap til it was good and clean. Then I was sent to my room. Mother-Fucker is a bad word. I knew it. Nigger was just as bad. But like Mother-Fucker, I didn't know what the word meant.

My dad said the word sometimes. Whenever we moved the two blocks from one apartment to the next, Dad said it was because "there's too many niggers on this block." I knew there was something or someone that was a nigger and it was a bad word, bad enough to get soaped for saying it and bad enough to make us move. After my father nearly ripped my hair from my head, I knew for the first time what the word actually meant. And I wondered why my dad didn't like my friends. Just cuz of their color? Heck, my father loved Ernie Banks and he was black, too.

Mr. O'Brien

My dad just got back from the sanitarium five days ago. He spent most of the week sitting by an open front room window sucking in the city air. We're heading up to Popp's Tavern and Dad isn't walking so good. His legs don't seem like they want to move. When we get to 79th and Racine, Tommy White comes running up to me, a crazy look on his face. He always talks kinda funny. Most people can't understand Tommy, but I can. He's got a hole up inside his mouth. Once, after I gave him my Ron Santo baseball card, Tommy opened his mouth up wide and let me have a look. I needed a flashlight to see the hole. It's at the very top of the inside of his mouth, 'bout the size of a dime. Tommy's gonna make his communion this year. Everyone in the neighborhood is hopin that the white wafer'll get stuck to the roof of Tommy's mouth and stay put, so we can all understand him. "God might be planning just such a miracle," my mom says and smiles, whenever she talks about Tommy.

"id nyou ear 'out ickie O'rien," Tommy says slowly. My dad sucks on his cigarette and shakes his head.

"What about Dickie?" I ask. Dad looks at me with raised eyebrows, amazed at my interpretation skills.

"hey hot im ast ight at da ark." Tommy's face goes limp. He stares a hole into his black Cons. "e's ead."

I look at my dad. "Dickie O'Brien's dead, Dad?" Tommy nods his head.

"Yah," my father says with barely a sliver of emotion on his face. "Tommy's right. Dickie's dead." Tommy keeps nodding.

"Who shot 'im?" I ask.

Tommy starts to speak. My dad jambs his cigarette between his lips and shakes both hands at Tommy, his slender fingers fluttering back and forth like the wings of a wounded bird.

"Thanks Tommy. Shove off, now. We gotta go," my father says. Tommy leaves. I watch him. He crosses the street and races up to another man on the sidewalk, just across from us. I can't quite make out who the man is cuz he has a Sox hat pulled down over his face. Whoever he is, he's about to find out about Dickie O'Brien. If he's a skilled interpreter, like me.

"Who shot 'im?" I ask again.

"Who do ya think?" Dad says through twisted lips. My father shoes his cigarette into the sidewalk, taking great pains to ensure the fire is out. "Dickie's dead and it's a damn shame." He stares briefly up into the crisp, blue sky, pulls another cigarette out and lights it as we walk. I don't toss the ball into the sky anymore and I don't talk either. I just think about Dickie. He was always nice to me when he saw me. He liked to pat me on the head and call me "Freckle Boy." Dickie was the best guy on St. Leo's basketball team. My brothers took me to a couple of his games. I love that tiny gym, stacked on the third floor of the school. Dickie was all set to go to DePaul on a basketball scholarship. He had a good jump shot and he was a dead eye from the free throw line. Least that's what the men at Popp's always said about him. And from what I saw, they were right.

As we near Popp's, there's a huge crowd in front--bigger than any I'd seen at opening time. I can see some of the faces but not most of 'em. Mr. Popp pushes the door open and the men file in. My dad works his way into his seat near the end of the bar. I stand behind him 'cuz all the stools are filled up by the bar men. Mr. Popp sticks a beer, a shot of whiskey and a shorty glass in front of my father and he remembers my Pepsi, too. Dad fills the shorty with beer. Mr. Popp doesn't pull his eye out today, though. He ties his white apron around his waist and stares about the tavern at the men. His face is blank. Mr. Popp seems miles away.

"Hey Mr. Popp aren't you gonna--" I start. He looks at me and smiles. Now, that's the Mr. Popp I know.

"Oh," he says digging into his eye socket, "here you go young, Master Dennis." He pulls out his fake eye and walks towards me and my father. The eye slips through his fingers as he nears us and bounces like a marble off the bar top. It hops into my dad's shorty glass. Dad stares at the eye as it whirls about in the golden fluid like a top spinning in slow motion. The eye is scary lookin in the glass. It's like it's two or three times bigger than normal and it's starin right at me. I wonder why it's so big and I keep thinkin it's gonna explode, so I turn away. But when I turn away, there's Mr. Popp standin right in front of me and I stare directly into the gaping hole in his face. It all happened so fast, I didn't get a chance to turn away or count, like usual. I just stare at that hole. But I didn't puke this time. When Mr. Popp turns away, I do the same. My eyes fall directly on Mr. Lassandrello. He's here and early. That's not a good sign. I glance back at my dad. He's fishing for the eye in his glass, using his two index fingers like a tweezers. It works. He wedges the eyeball between the backs of both index fingers, lays the eye softly on the bar top, and dries it off with one of those tiny napkins that have the cheesy jokes on 'em. My dad then downs the beer from his shorty glass. I look to the left. On the stool at the far curve of the bar is Mr. O'Brien, Senior--Dickie's dad. He's a solid man, tall and well built. He's wearing a short-sleeved shirt. I can see his muscles, all veiny and hard. He looks like he belongs in a strong man magazine. Mr. O'Brien tries hard not to smile whenever he sees me, but he's such a happy guy, he can't help but smile. His square face is perfect in every way cept for what hides behind his lips. I don't know what Mr. O'Brien does for work, but his teeth look like he chews on cement for a living. He's not smiling today, though. Definitely not. He's accepting shot after shot from those sitting all around him. I wanna hug Mr. O'Brien and tell him how sad I am about Dickie. I don't. I just stand behind my dad and keep my ears open.

"Fred, Fred, take care of that, will ya?" Mr. Simms says, pointing toward Mr. Popp's eye.

"What?" Mr. Popp says.

"Your eye, your eye. Cover the damn thing up, will ya?" Mr. Simms says. "I came hear to drink my beer, not to toss my breakfast." Mr. Popp shakes his head, grabs the patch from the cash register drawer and slips the patch in place.

"Sorry, I didn't—"

"No problem, Freddy." Mr. Simms takes a small sip of beer. "I'd forget my own prick if it wasn't sewn to me." They both share a laugh but not too loud. They don't want to offend Mr. O'Brien.

I snag a few nickels from my dad and go over by the bowling machine. It's right behind where Mr. O'Brien is sitting. I put a nickel in and play. I play real slow.

"We gotta do somethin," Mr. Farrel says. "We can't let 'em get away with this shit."

"Dey'll own the neighborhood soon," Mr. Naughton hollers.

"Hell," Mr. Farrel says, "they own the friggin neighborhood now." He takes a long drink from his bottle. "They're everywhere."

"I'm not afraid to say it," Mr. D'Amico says. "I talked it over with the wife." Mr. D'Amico's bald head is smooth and tan. He's one of the few non-Irish that my father actually likes. "We're gonna move."

All eyes in the group flash towards Mr. O'Brien. He continues his silence, staring at the bar top, downing shot after shot, taking time only to breath.

"Don't move Dom," Mr. Farrel screeches. His face is wrinkled like a bulldog. "That's just what they want." He swigs on his beer. "Too many have already gone. That's parta the problem. But we haven't gone. We can still make this neighborhood ours."

"Ditto, Dom. Ditto," Mr. Naughton says.

I roll a black ball down the lane. I get eight pins. The ball is smaller than a 16-inch Clincher softball but bigger than a baseball. It's black in color. Very, very black. I know who they're talking about, even if they don't use the bad word.

"I got older kids," Mr. D'Amico says, "kids who are out at the parks all the time. Hell, little Dom was at the park with Dickie when it happened. I'm lucky he's not a goner, too." Mr. D'Amico stares at Mr. O'Brien. "I don't want to take any more chances. I don't want to wait any more."

Mr. Carroll walks into the bar. He cranes his neck about, his eyes moving rapidly. He then walks directly toward Mr. O'Brien. Hands return glasses to the bar top, stools are adjusted, and all eyes follow Mr. Carroll.

"We got the fuckin nigger who killed Dickie," Mr. Carroll declares proudly. Feet stomp, hands clap, and mouths cheer. I decide to keep count of the number of times I hear that bad word. One. All eyes are pointed at Mr. Carroll. He's still in uniform, his starchy, blue shirt buttoned almost all the way to the top, his shiny badge aglow from the overhead lights. I look at his gun. It's tucked neatly in its holster like a baby under covers, with his head and feet sticking out. Mr. Carroll let me hold the gun once, when he had a bunch of beers in him. I think he said it was a Colt .45. Mr. O'Brien continues to drink. He doesn't even look at Mr. Carroll.

"He's at the station right now, singing like the yellow fuckin canary nigger that he is." Two. Mr. O'Brien keeps starin at the bar top. "OB, did you hear what I said?" Mr. Carroll nudges his way next to Mr. O'Brien. He puts his right hand on Mr. O'Brien's shoulder. "We got 'im OB. You hear me? We got the fuckin nigger." Three.

"Fine work, Marty," Mr. O'Brien finally mumbles. His words aren't too clear and I can hardly make out his brogue. Mr. O'Brien doesn't take his eyes off the bar top. Instead, he stares at the shot glass in his right hand, filled to the white line with whiskey. He pushes the glass back and forth on the bar top in front of him. The bar top is shiny and smooth and the glass glides over it like a puck on ice. Mr. O'Brien never even spills a drop. Mr. Carroll's face is tight, disappointed. Mr. Farrel pulls him back and whispers something in his ear. Mr. Carroll shrugs his shoulders.

"See ya later guys," he says, wagging his head. "I gotta get back to the station." Mr. Carroll walks for the door swiftly amidst back slaps and cheers of "good work, Marty." My father still has an Old Style, a shot glass and a shorty glass in front of him on the bar top. Each one will get filled or replaced as the day moves along. That much I know is certain.

"When's the wake and funeral?" Mr. Everett asks. I like Mr. Everett. I told ya 'bout him before. He's the tiny guy with the pointy beard and well-aimed punches. Mr. Farrell presses his "Shush" finger to his lips. He waves Mr. Everett over. They move away from Mr. O'Brien and stand directly next to me. I roll another black ball down the lane, my eyes intent on the lane, my ears reaching for Mr. Farrell's whispering lips. "They have to complete the autopsy and all that kinda jazz. That'll probably take a few days. He'll probably wake 'im on Wednesday. Two days worth, of course, and then have the funeral on Friday."

Mr. Everett drinks his beer. He's a Hamms from the land of sky blue waters man. "Dickie could fill the parlor for five days if it was allowed."

Mr. Farrell nods his head in agreement. "Fuckin niggers," he breaths lightly. Four.

I roll the ball at the reset pins and score a strike. "Ya-hoo, Ya-hoo," I holler, my arms raised above my head, my legs bouncing up and down. My first strike ever. In all my time comin to Popp's. My first strike. I can't believe it. I been tryin and tryin and finally I got it. As I turn and look at my father, all life in the bar again screeches to a halt. I feel eyes upon me. The bar is silent, like when Mr. Carroll came in. Glasses again rest on the bar top and chairs are aimed at me. I look to my father for support. His lips and eyes are pinched. He looks like he wants to bite me. I wanna cry. My eyes race across the faces of Sheehy, Everett, Farrell, Callahan, D'Amico, Mueller, Byrnes, Naughton, Cassidy, Smith, Murphy, Simms, Dunleavy, Hodorowicz, Walsh, Moore, Freyer, Keane, Klein, O'Malley, Moran, Lassandrello, O'Brien, McGuire.

My eyes stop moving when I see Mr. O'Brien's face. I look no further. He has swung around on his stool. His back is turned to the bar top now and he's starin at me. I tuck my chin to my chest and stare at the wet floor.

"Ah, dat was a fine strike," Mr. O'Brien says. His brogue is thick and I can understand him now. I lift my eyes. Mr. O'Brien's smiling at me. I smile back. "As fine a strike as ever I've seen." His sky blue eyes dart about the bar erasing the looks of doom on the other bar men's faces. "Why it wouldn't surprise me one bit if you became a championship bowler when you're older. Is dat what ya want to be when you get older, a bowler?"

I shake my head. "I wanna be a ballplayer, for the Cubs." The bar men smile and laugh. "I have my mitt and ball here."

"Is dat right? Well, go get 'em, lad. Lemme see your arm." I grab my ball and mitt from the bar top, next to my father and Mr. Popp's eye. Mr. O'Brien climbs off his stool and the men part around him. He crouches into a catcher's position. "Show me your fast one, Denny. Lemme have your best." I'm about thirty feet away from Mr. O'Brien.

"Ya sure, Mr. O'Brien?"

"Yes. Yes. Show me the dark one." He smiles at me. I return his smile, rare back and fire a strike at his face. He catches the ball with his bare hands. "Oh, that was a fine heater." He throws the ball back. "Throw me one more."

Again I lift my left leg, lean back and fire another strike. Again Mr. O'Brien snares the ball with his bare hands. He then drops the ball to the ground and shakes his hands. "Ooh. Ooh.

Dat one stung, Denny-me-lad. No more. You'll break me hands." He smiles one last cement-chewing-smile.

I look about the bar. All the men are smiling. Mr. O'Brien grabs the ball, flips it back to me and returns to his stool. He's still facing me. I set the ball and mitt on the bowling table. Mr. O'Brien's legs are spread wide, his shoes resting on the bottom of the stool pipe. His eyes are still on me. I walk between his legs, stick my face in his chest and throw my arms as far around his big back as they'll go.

"I'm sorry about what happened to Dickie," I say. Mr. O'Brien sits limp for a moment but then wraps his muscular arms around me. He says nothing. He sits still for a moment, but then his chest begins to shake. It then rumbles. Large tears fall upon my hair and neck. The sound he releases is of a pain-stricken giant. I hold on to him and shake with him. I will not let go. I will hold him for as long as he would like. He shakes and sobs and shakes and sobs. I don't wanna let go and neither does he. The sounds keep comin and so do the tears. His screeches then slow down and become gentle sighs. The water stops fallin on my back. Mr. O'Brien releases me and I let go as well.

"God bless you, little one," he says softly. I look up at Mr. O'Brien. The tears carved numerous passageways down his handsome face. He erases these tearful tracks with the backs of his hands and sets his giant right paw on my flaming hair. He strokes my hair and runs his eyes around the bar, his eyes growing more intense with each face they find.

"Dis is why you need to leave dis neighborhood," Mr. O'Brien says, still stroking my hair. "You all have kids. The neighborhood aint what it used to be. It's a dangerous, deadly place. We all know that now." He stares at my father. "I hafta live with my decision to stay. Dom's gettin smart. You guys should all go." He wipes the tears again from his eyes and then rips through his own hair with both hands. "Go now," Mr. O'Brien screams, "while ya still have children to love." Mr.

O'Brien looks at me and sobs lightly. I stare at the floor. "Goodbye, little Denny." He pats my head once more, climbs off his stool and walks briskly for the door, the whiskeys he drank not showing in his gait.

Mr. Farrell slides into Mr. O'Brien's seat. He huddles with his crew and keeps talkin about the pluses and minuses of leaving and staying in the neighborhood. For me, I never wanna leave. We moved a couple a times the past few years, moving blocks at a time, but we stayed in the same neighborhood. I go back and forth between my father and the bowling game for another three hours. The bad word is said another 37 times for a grand total of 41. Mr. Farrell's the definite leader in times said. At 3:30, my dad slides off his stool. We're leaving early, which isn't the usual case. I wonder if my dad's out of money.

"See ya, Fred," my dad says. He waves to the others and we move toward the door. Mr. Popp gives me the thumbs up sign and then sticks his eyeball back in place.

"Hold it Foley," a voice barks. I know that voice. I turn and see Mr. Lassandrello standing beside his stool like a gunslinger ready for the draw. He lumbers slowly towards my dad, the booze slowing his feet. My dad is still facing the door. They're only about twenty feet apart. Here we go again. My father and Mr. Lassandrello hate each other. They have to club each other every few months or so in order to continue living. It's something to do with my mother from their high school days. All eyes are on my father. He slips his hand quietly and quickly into my mitt and grabs the league ball. He spins and fires a rocket with his left hand, or the hand of the devil--as the nuns call it. The ball hits Mr. Lassandrello square in the forehead and bounces directly back to me. I field the grounder and hand it back to my dad. I'm hopin he'll plunk him in the face again. Mr. Lassandrello seems to be sleeping while standing up. I can see the imprint of the ball's stitches on his forehead. All I can think of are cartoons. Surely, Mr. Lassandrello must be seein stars dancin all around his skull, like Brutus—whenever Popeye socks him one over the head. Mr. Lassandrello finally crumples to the floor and the bar men all laugh and slap their knees. My father sticks the league back in my mitt. We walk out the door and head for home.

Holy Cross Hospital--Day 4

I finally took my first crap today. It wasn't much of a loaf but it sure was stinky as all hell. But the worst part of it was, I had to hand the bed pan over to the cute nurse. Where are all the whale-sized nurses when you really need them? Probably munchin on a Twinkie somewhere. Yum, yum, cream filling. The cute nurse's name is Tracie. She's been real nice to me. She's got a pimple-free, perky face and a nice smile. Those teeth fill up her mouth but they're not too, too big. Her blond hair reaches almost to her shoulders and it's kinda shaggy. But the best part of her is her butt. Ooh wee, do I like to watch her wiggle away after she gives me the once over. She could use a little help in the chest department, but that's okay. I'm definitely a butt man first. I like talkin to Tracie. She just walked across the stage at St. Xavier College this year, so she's only about six or seven years older than me. I can't wait till I get to college. I hope there's lotsa Tracies there. I go to St. Laurence, an all-boys Catholic high school. Queen of Peace, the all-girls Catholic school, is right next door but all those girls look the same with their white shirts, plaid skirts and knee socks. There's not a good lookin girl like Tracie around for miles.

They started me in on regular food today. It's not great stuff, but it is food. It went right through me. That's why I had to fill that bed pan. I'm back on the brainwaves with the old man. He's been lettin me in on his thoughts again. It's real weird. It's like he's in some far away fantasy land. There's waterfalls everywhere and birds and blue skies and horses with wings and smiley-faced people too. He's not dreamin. His eyes are wide open and he keeps blinkin. Maybe God's advance men are showin him where he's going. It looks like a nice place, wherever it is.

Later on in the day, I ask the old guy about his tattoo. Is that an Army Ranger tattoo? I say, pointin at his arm. He smiles and says, Yes. Then he tells me a little bit about his days fighting in France. The old man was a Ranger. That's awfully damn cool. I wanna know more but I stop with the questions when I can see that it hurts the old guy a lot to talk.

Just before I went to sleep for the night, the old guy cracked another smile when Tracie carried away my bed pan with the you-know-what in it. I swear. He took off his mask and smiled. I cut loose a big grin myself and chuckled too. Tracie heard me. She spun around quick and looked my way with tight eyes. I erased all semblance of laughter from my face and stretched out my right arm like I was yawning. I even made the yawning sound to be extra convincing. Tracie seemed to accept that. Her eyes flared back to normal and she turned and walked away. The old guy dozed off before me. I can tell that he's only got a few more days left in him. I can feel it. I just don't want to see him die alone.

The Snow of '67

The great snow of '67 fell on January 26th and 27th. In total, God dumped about two-feet of flakes on Chicago. Schools were closed. Yippee! And the city was at a stand still. So what! We were still a family then--all of us under one roof.

Snowdrifts climbed as tall as six feet in the back yard, below the porch. It was too much to resist. All of us kids--even little Donna--took turns jumpin off the second-floor banister, punching hole after hole into the white blanket with our bodies. Dad watched all the activities from the porch. He smiled and laughed and even slung a few snowballs at us. He was sober that day.

Later in the day on the 27th, while all us kids were slurping our dinner soup at the kitchen table, Franky "The Hocker" Figlio climbed up the back porch and smushed his lips against our kitchen window. He then banged away on the storm door. Franky was wearin a furry, Russian hat that made his tiny head look huge, and a brown Corduroy coat with no holes in it. We called him "The Hocker" cuz he could spit out the best goobers you ever saw. If you told Franky to mix up a red goober for you, he'd suck way down in his throat and then spit out a goober that was as red as a fire truck. He did that by somehow getting blood into the mix. If it was a green goober you wanted, Franky would toss out a goober filled up with green snot. No one knew Franky's secrets. I only hoped that I would be able to spit like him when I got older. Johnny popped the door open. He and Franky were in the same grade.

"You gotta come down to the can factory," Franky said.

"Why?" Johnny said.

"Man, there's snow mountains everywhere. We're havin a war. A huge war."

Johnny turned back and looked at Mom. We were done with our soup so she gave us the nod. Dad did too. Within seconds we slid back in our coats and snow suits, and slid out the door. We marched the block-and-a-half to the parking lot of the Continental Can factory at 76th and Racine, and once we got there we knew that Hocker wasn't lyin. The snow crew had cleared the whole lot. In doing so, they created a Winter wonderland. Hills reaching fifteen feet and more stretched into the sky. What a sight. Word spread quickly amongst the kids in the neighborhood. In a snap, the lot was overflowing with young bodies dressed in snow suits, black rubber boots and stocking caps. Every family in the neighborhood seemed to be represented. A King of the Hill competition started. The McIlhernes stood atop the tallest hill for quite a while. Until it was our turn. All six of us stormed the hill and tossed the McIlhernes off. They were no problem. We then sunk our feet in stone atop that hill and refused to be dethroned. All night long, we beat back family after family, including the Murphys, and they had 14, flattening everyone that got in our way. Sure we took some good blows ourselves, but we never gave up. Of course, it didn't hurt having Tim on our side either. He was only 13 at the time but he already had the body and strength of Charles Atlas. Anyone who penetrated our line of defense found Tim as the final soldier. And away they went, sailing and rolling down the snowy hill. At day's end, when we were the only kids left, we slid down the hill we owned and strutted like snow-covered peacocks back to our apartment. Mom made some hot chocolate for us and we all sat in the kitchen, Dad included, and held a brag session about our King of the Hill exploits. Dad said little while we told our tale but he held a proud grin on his face the whole time. Everything was normal. But things would never be like that again.

Five Quarters

It was Superball time again. I was with Willie in the alley behind my apartment. Just the two of us. No Winston. I liked it most when it was just Willie and me. Sure, I liked Winston but when he was with us, it seemed I spent mosta my time breakin up fights between him and Willie and sayin 'No' to all his crazy ideas. Willie was my best friend and I was his. We just never told Winston that.

Earlier in the day, before Willie came to call on me, my mom told me that we were gonna move from our apartment to some place called the suburbs. She said it wouldn't be for almost a month yet. She said she didn't want to move during the school year, but it was time to go. I didn't wanna move. Especially not since we were leavin St. Sabina's altogether.

"Why, Ma?" I asked her. "Why do we hafta move?"

Her eyebrows shot up and she nodded her head toward the front room. "Ask him. It's his bright idea." So I marched into the front room and did just that.

"How come you wanna move, Dad?"

He was sittin on the couch, his feet kicked up on a chair, his face hidden behind the newspaper. "It's just time to move. That's all." And that was all he said. He didn't even put the newspaper down to talk.

Willie and I took turns slammin the Superball into the cement and chasing it down. We played garage ball too, where you pitched the Superball at the garage door and watched it ricochet back and forth offa that garage and the garage on the other side of the alley--until the ball just got tired and stopped movin. As we played, I kept tryin to find a good time to tell Willie I was movin, but the time never seemed right. When the Superball got stuck in the gutter on the garage, I figured it was about as good a time as any.

"Hey Willie," I said, "I got somethin I gotta—"

Just then, five boys turn the corner of the alley. Their strides were long and fast. They were up on us before we could move. Two boys stood in front of Willie and me and three stood behind us. I knew all of 'em from school but I only knew one by name. They were all white kids and they were a year ahead of us at St. Sabina's.

"I'm gonna knock the snot outta you, Foley," the tall one in front of me said. His dark hair was cut tight to his scalp and he had me by a few inches and many pounds.

"Me too," said the kid next to him.

"Me three," and "Me four" said two voices from behind us, and then Jimmy Riordan said, "Me five."

I didn't know why these guys were out to get me. Sure, I'd been gettin in a few fights at school, but I didn't fight with any of these guys. I stared at the bristles atop the tall one's head, tryin to figure it out, and then it came to me. This was a big-brother payback. I punched Jimmy Riordan's little brother, Luke, in the gut at recess two days before, and Luke spent the rest of that recess cryin his little eyes out like the sissy he was. Jimmy was here to pay me back, only he wasn't much good with his fists. I could take him and he knew it. That's why he brought his buddies along.

I balled my hands into fists and stared at the nose just below those dark bristles. That's where I decided my first punch would go. I was gonna strike first. My brothers taught me that much. Sure, I'd get beat-up, but with Willie there, we stood a chance of gettin some good punches in--before they finally creamed us. I was about to fire my right fist at that nose when Willie spoke.

"Hey, y'all got any money on ya?"

"What?" the tall one said, his face twisted, tryin to make sense of the question.

Wrinkles climbed across my face, too. I was wonderin what Willie was doin.

"All I did was ax if y'all had any money on ya," Willie said.

That was a crazy question to ask for two reasons. One. None of these kids had any money on 'em. If they did, they wouldn't have been in the alley chasing me down. They would've been at Mr. Moran's store buying some penny candy. Two. Why ask a question like that at a time like this, when we were about to get whipped good?

"I aint got no money on me," the tall one said.

"Me neither," said Jimmy Riordan. The other three stayed quiet.

Willie smiled a wide smile, looked my way, and then dug into his right pants pocket. He fiddled around in there for a bit and then pulled out his hand. It was squeezed into a fist. He opened his fist and layin there in the palm of his hand was a clump of quarters--five in all--sparkling away in the sunlight. A quarter was like a gold piece to us back then. With a quarter, you could buy a pack of baseball cards, some pop and Kayos, and all the penny candies you could swallow. Five quarters could definitely get you some good stuff.

"I was just thinkin," Willie said, "I aint got much use for these here quarters." Again he made a fist but it was a loose fist, like he was tryin to leave room for the quarters to breath. He shook his fist and the coins jingle-jangled. The three boys that stood behind us moved around in front with the others. Willie again opened his hand. All five of the boys were starin at the coins.

"If you don't want dem coins, I'll take 'em," the tall one said. He shot his hand towards Willie's quarters. Willie again turned his hand into rock, protecting the gold.

"This is the way it is," Willie said. "Y'all can each have a quarter, but only if y'all promise not to beat up Dennis."

It didn't take much time for the answers to come. Okays flew outta five mouths, and then five hands with skinny, white fingers opened wide in front of Willie's black face. So much for the big brother payback. Willie dropped a quarter into each hand. The five boys then made their way down the alley in silence, starin at the quarters in their hands like they were diamonds, and turned in the direction of Mr. Moran's store. They were, no doubt, ready to fill their bellies full of pop and candy.

Once the boys were outta sight, Willie and me rolled a garbage can over to where the Superball was stuck. I climbed atop the garbage can and fished the ball outta the gutter. I flipped the ball to Willie and he slammed it into the ground. He chased the ball down and I followed him.

"Where'd you get all that money, Willie?"

"I always carries that money." He rolled the Superball between his fingers. "My momma and gram-momma both been givin me quarters on each of my last few birt'days. I don't like spendin 'em, though. I likes the feel of 'em in my pocket. So I just kept 'em in there for when I needed 'em." Willie flipped me the ball. "Let 'er ride," he said.

I slammed the ball into the ground and Willie and I chased it down. I handed him the ball.

"Thanks Willie." I wanted to say more but my mouth just wouldn't move. My brain got stuck cuz I was searchin for the right words. There just had to be somethin more to say to someone who spent his life's savings to keep me from gettin beat-up. I only wished my dad had been there to see the whole thing. Maybe he'd change his mind about movin then.

"No problem," Willie said. Then he reached into his pants pocket and pulled out a fist, just like before. "Guess what?" Willie shook his fist from side to side in front of me, the grin still on his face. I just shook my head to and fro. "I got one mo' fo' us." He opened his hand and there laying in his palm was one last shiny quarter. "Let's go spennit." And so we did.

Willie and I walked the block-and-a-half to Mr. Moran's store, bouncing the Superball as we moved. We both went inside and Willie bought a pack of baseball cards, two Kayos and some penny candy. Once we were outside, I told Willie right away that me and my family was movin. If ever there was an upside down smile, Willie had it on his face right then and there. I felt the exact same way. Willie never asked why we were movin. We just sat down outside the store, our backs pressed against the cool brick wall, and drank our Kayos and ate our candy and read the stats on the backside of the cards we got. We didn't say much the whole time. And when we were done with our snacks, we just stayed right there and watched the people and cars and sun go by, neither of us quite ready to head for home.

Naked Ladies

Richie Gannon showed me my first naked lady picture. He was a fourth-grader at St. Sabina's and I was in second. I was a big kid--tall and skinny for my age--so when I wasn't with Willie, I hung around with some of the older kids, like Richie. The lady in the picture was all by herself, kneeling on some sort of wild animal skin, something she probably picked up on one of her safari hunts in Africa. She had starchy, golden hair that laid flat across her shoulders. Her hands were on the sides of her boobs and she smushed 'em together. I don't know why she smushed her boobs together, but she musta liked doing it cuz she wore a big blinding smile between her fire-engine-red lips. A little patch of fur covered her between the legs spot. I didn't know what that was all about and I didn't really care much either. I just liked lookin at her boobs. I wondered what they would look like if she just took her hands off of 'em, just for a minute. Richie showed me lots of naked lady pictures after that, but I'll always remember that first lady, even though I never knew her name.

About a week or so before I moved, I was drinking a pop with Tom Fitzgibbons and Mickey Moran, just outside of Mickey's dad's store, when Richie waved to us from across the street. We all knew what that meant. We were more than happy to see what Richie had for us. I bottomed out my pop, stuck it inside the crate outside of the store, and hurried across the street with Tom and Mickey. Richie pulled out a picture from his back pocket, a picture the likes of which none of us had ever seen, and unfolded it. In the picture, a naked lady was laying down on a bed and a naked man was laying directly on top of her. They were facing each other and there was nothing between them. It was like they were sewn together.

"How ya like that?" Richie said, winking at us. I said nothing. I just stared at the picture.

"Where'd you get it?" Tom asked, his eyes not straying from the picture as he spoke.

"Found it in my old man's work desk out in the garage." All of our eyes were still fixed on the picture. Then, without warning, Richie folded the picture back into fours and stuffed it into his pocket. He smiled. "Pretty cool, huh?"

"Yah," Mickey said quickly.

"Real cool," Tom added. I just nodded my head and watched the older guys.

Richie tapped his back pocket, the spot that held the object of our fancy. "I just wanted you guys to see that cuz it's somethin special." He slowed his words down and leaned in close to us. "That's what you do when you love somebody. You climb on top of 'em like that."

I moved away from those guys just after Christmas, but I never forgot those pictures and I never forgot Richie's words either.

The Fish House

Hometown was the name of the new place we moved to. No more Willie and Winston. Mom said I'd make new friends. We lived in a tiny white house that was cut in two. Mom called it a duplex. Maybe if we lived in both sides of the duplex, we woulda had enough room. As it was, it seemed we couldn't take two steps without crawling on top of one another. Dad was with us at first, but then he went off to the sanitarium again. When he got out, he didn't come back with us. He stayed in a place of his own somewhere, and Mom never said why. Hometown was a strange place--very different from the St. Sabina's neighborhood. There were no two-flats or three-flats and there were no brick bungalows either. Hometown was a tiny village--just past the Southern edge of Chicago--made up of nothin but white, frame and aluminum-sided duplexes, all one level houses just like ours. And most everything else in that town was white, too: garages, sheds, picket fences, and faces.

Hometown was the very first place we lived for a long while--a whole year--without Dad. Dad did, however, pop by on occasion. He paid me a visit just two weeks before I was to make my First Holy Communion. He took me back to Popp's Tavern. It was good to see Mr. Popp again. He kept his eye in its socket the whole time and I didn't ask him to take it out. Dad drank his usual shots and beers and we didn't talk much. That was fine with me, though. I had enough Pepsis to make me happy and, besides, my 8-year-old brain was filled with thoughts of my impending religious experience. I was so ready for that day. In all honesty, I could care less about receiving that white, cardboard-tasting host, the EMBODIMENT OF JESUS CHRIST. Envelopes. That's all I cared about. Envelopes. At my Communion party, I knew I'd get loads of envelopes filled to the gills with paper thin goodies, if ya know what I mean. I had learned the lessons directed my way by the nuns at Our Lady of Loretto School and I was ready to be made holy. I was also ready to be made rich.

My dad had other plans for me, though; another lesson he thought I should learn. When we left Mr. Popp, Dad had quite a good one goin. We climbed into his car and headed for home. As my father drove, I found it hard to understand how he kept his license. He ran a stop sign at 76th and Racine, another at 76th and Loomis, and he avoided the red light at 79th and Loomis by cutting through the White Castle parking lot. That didn't bother me much, though. Since Dad wasn't around much, that meant I didn't get many chances to ride in his Corvair. God, I loved that car--with the engine in the rear and all. I'd like to meet the guy who dreamt up that idea. But Dad was tearin up the clutch with his whiskey feet as he drove, and the engine screamed each time he shifted into the next gear. Thankfully, he finally gave the engine a rest, curbing the Corvair outside the All Seasons Pet Shop at 87th and Honore. I was a bit surprised.

"C'mon," my dad said, "let's go in." This wasn't our usual pet store. I hadn't noticed it, but my dad had looped around and had driven many miles into foreign territory. I looked at him with stupid eyes. "C'mon," he barked. I obeyed and followed him into the pet shop. Once inside, my dad worked the aisles staring at the assorted items atop the solid wooden shelves. I wandered over by the live animals hoping to find a snake inhaling a tiny white mouse or something equally as gross. What I found was even better. A pair of mating hamsters. My soon-to-be-holy eyes were glued to these creatures. The man hamster was atop the lady hamster. He sunk his tiny paws into her side and moved back and forth violently. They had wee grins on their fuzzy, little faces and all of their furry neighbors stood nearby and watched. When they finished, I was disappointed it didn't last longer. The lady hamster probably felt the same way. She was no longer smiling. The man hamster was.

I searched the aisles for my dad. I found him smirking away at a blue and white ceramic fish house, suitable for insertion in a fish tank. It was a Victorian structure complete with two turrets, authentic-looking fish-scale siding, and a lovely wrap-around porch. The fish house had open front and side doors for the fish to swim through. My father shook the smile from his lips when he noticed me watchin him.

"Let's go," he barked again. I followed my father to the check-out counter and we stood there, empty handed. The bell above the entry door jingled as the last customer left the store.

"Don't ya have any bigger bags of seed then those?" My dad pointed at the 5 and 10 pound bags of bird seed stacked a few feet away on the floor.

Now I took care of all our pets at the time. We had one rabbit, six gold fish, a canary, and a lizard named Chauncey. We had an abundance of food for all the pets at home--bird seed included. I was about to tell my father this when the shop owner spoke.

"We do have some 25 pound bags."

"Really," my dad said in a fakey sort a way. "I didn't see any."

"They're in the basement."

"Oh, all right." My dad ran his left hand through his hair. "Gimme two a those big bags," he said, flashing a peace sign.

The shop owner's eyes lit up. "Sure. Give me a sec," he said quickly, a slanted grin spreading across his mug. "I'll bring those right up for ya." It wasn't much of a sale but it was somethin, I guess. It had to be if it made the shop owner that happy. Just then, a strange, non-pet-like odor mingled with the air. I couldn't help but think that the owner figured he played my dad for a sap. He was about to unload the stale seed that, no doubt, had been squatting in his basement for many years.

Yep, he definitely figured my dad for a sap. That's what I smelled in the air. He was dead wrong, though.

The shopkeeper opened the basement door and slowly worked his feet down the many steps. My dad immediately sprang into action, bolting to the aisle where he had earlier eyeballed the Victorian fish house. He plucked it from the shelf, ran back to me, grabbed me by my collar, and pulled me out the door. We jumped into the Corvair and raced away. The car seemed to hum smoothly the rest of the way home.

At home, I watched as my father inserted the ceramic house inside the fish tank. He then stooped over and circled his head about the tank admiring his new trinket from all angles. John and Tim also came over for a peek. I saw them whisper to one another, nod their heads at the tank, and then giggle. They stopped when my father glared at them.

I had enough. Don't ask me why, but suddenly I was tired. It was only 4:30 in the afternoon but I was dead tired. I said my prayers and then laid down for a good nap. I didn't have one. Huge goldfish with bulging eyes swam through my head as I slept. These huge fish kept going to the homes of other fish and stealing their clothes. I was only too happy to awaken. My father was already gone. Back to his place, I guessed. I immediately walked over to the fish tank and stared at the new ceramic house. The words MEN and WOMEN were now scribbled in indelible black marker above the two open doors, and I watched as the fish swam happily throughout the rooms of their new home.

Sex

I didn't like Hometown much at first. I missed Willie and Winston and I even missed seeing their old gramma and her half-smoked cigs. But once I got to know Suzy Egan, all that changed. Like me, Suzy was a second-grader. She lived with her mom and brothers just around the corner from our duplex and we went to the same school. When Sister Agnes, my new teacher, introduced me as the new kid to the class, the first thing I noticed was Suzy, smiling at me from her front row seat. She had green eyes, shiny teeth like the people on the Pepsodent commercials, and stringy blond hair that was cut in a straight line above her shoulders. I smiled right back at Suzy that first day and things moved along quick from there. There's no other way to say it, other than to say it. Is it possible to fall in love when you're only nine? Whatever love--or like--was to me then, I felt it for Suzy. I felt for Suzy like I felt for my own mom.

Most times, Suzy and I hung out in the tree fort in the back yard. The family that rented the place before us built it and didn't bother tearin it down when they left. So we put it to good use. Suzy was quite the reader. While I busied myself with my Superman comic books in the fort, Suzy turned the pages of a book by some guy named e.e. cummings. He was her favorite. I knew then Suzy was special. Heck, I never cracked open a book or at least tried not to, and there was Suzy with Mr. cummings' book always in front of her face. I figured then she was ahead of her times. She read all of her favorite poems to me. By Summer's end, Suzy took to spellin her name--suzy, with a small "s". She helped me learn the words to Mr. cummings' "maggie and millie and molly and may," and "Buffalo Bill's." When my Cubs failed to win the pennant, as usual, it was suzy's reading of Mr. cummings' "nobody loses all the time" that made me laugh and forget about the loss. But I had nothin I could give back to suzy--nothin good like that to share. All I could do was climb the stupid elm tree on a daily basis to pledge my like for suzy.

"suzy, I like you all the way from the ground up to here," I'd say, standing on a tree branch while holding my arm straight out as a marker.

"That's pretty high, Dennis," suzy would say.

"Yep."

"That's alotta like, right?"

"Yep." Each day I climbed a little higher on that elm, until, eventually, I ran out of branches to climb. From the tallest limb, I could see beyond the small, flat homes of Hometown. That's when flashes of Willie and Winston and St. Sabina's came roaring back. But no matter how hard or how far beyond I looked, I couldn't spot a single brick bungalow or two-flat, and there wasn't a black face around for miles. When I looked down, suzy was always there, lookin small and happy in my backyard, her mouth open, her teeth as white as the houses that surrounded us. I spent the remainder of the school year lookin for new ways to proclaim my like for suzy but found none. And that bothered me. A lot. I had to find somethin but my brain kept comin up with zeroes. So I kept searchin and searchin. And then it finally came to me one day while I was standin atop that tallest branch of the elm, starin out beyond the boundaries of Hometown: Richie Gannon's words, when he showed me that picture, "That's what you do when you love somebody. You climb on top of them like that." My problem was solved.

The garage was cleaner than it had ever been. Mom let Tim have a Kids-Only 8th grade graduation party in the garage and he and his friends spruced the place up real good. They tossed all the boxes of junk and stacks of magazines left behind by the former renters into garbage cans. The floor was given a new coat of multi-colored, psychedelic paint that was sliced into blue, red, yellow and orange foursies. A black light hung in the far corner away from the door and a poster of Jimmy Hendrix, panging on a guitar, floated on strings below the light. Peace signs were scribbled all over the inside walls of the garage and the remains of burnt incense slept inside old pop bottles. Tim's party was already done and over with and, as Tim had promised my mom, he made the place look better than it looked before the party. The garage was the perfect place for me and suzy.

I walked suzy into the garage and we stood in the center, at the very meeting point of the quadrants.

"suzy, you know I like you, right?" I started.

"Right," suzy answered swiftly. She sensed there was something major on my mind. She slid her gym shoe along the floor, stubbing it mostly into the red and yellow sections, waiting for me to speak. I tried to say more but I stopped. I was losin my nerve. I shook my head and mumbled. Nothing that made any sense came out.

"What is it?" suzy quizzed.

I stared at her emerald eyes and found my hand searching for, and finding, her hand. That was a first for me. Again I looked into her eyes. They were the same eyes that comforted me when I shared my secrets and when I talked about my dad. The words came easier then.

"It's just that I like you so much. I wish I could show you how much I like you."

"Climbin' the tree is fine with me," suzy said.

"Nah, there's more to it than that." I rubbed my hands across my face. "I've seen it." I then told suzy about the picture Richie Gannon showed me. Her eyes bugged wide and refused to blink. A lip-only smile scratched its way slowly across suzy's face. I took that as a yes. I walked over to the corner, turned my back to suzy and took off all my clothes except my Cons. suzy looked at me and quickly raced to the opposite corner where she took off her clothes. I covered my private with both hands, though there was little to cover, and suzy covered her lower area, too. We faced each other and stared. I could see past her hands. She didn't have any fur like the ladies in the nudity pictures and her boobs were no bigger than mine. When the starin was done, I grabbed suzy's arm and helped her lay down on the garage floor. The heat of Summer was upon us and yet the cement floor was ice-cold. I moved over suzy, on my hands and knees and looked down at her. Then slowly and softly I lowered my body directly onto her's. Half of suzy's body was pressed against the red section of the floor and half against the green section. We laid as still as dead men for a good two minutes. It seemed like hours. I kept lookin up to see if Mr. Hendrix was watchin. He wasn't. His eyes stayed focused on his guitar. suzy's body felt warm beneath mine and I enjoyed the closeness, though I knew it was sinful. At any moment, I expected one of my brothers to burst through the door with a priest or nun in tow. I was so scared I could barely feel or hear suzy's breath or my own.

"Think it's been long enough?" I finally asked.

"Sure do," suzy snapped.

"Me too." I jumped off of suzy and raced for my clothes. She did the same. Once dressed, we immediately ditched the garage and raced up to the tree house. We sat there for a few minutes, sayin nothin. It was an odd silence. I didn't like it. Not one bit. We were always easy to laugh and speak. But then suzy reached for double e and after a few poems, we were ourselves again.

"Do ya think we should ever do that again?" I asked.

"No," suzy muttered.

"Me neither," I said and then added, "but now you know how much I like you, right?"

"I know now, Dennis."

"Let's never tell anyone, okay suzy?"

"Deal," she said and then we shook hands. After the shake we continued to hold hands until the clock turned the blue sky into a black sky and the sun into a moon, and we were both called home for bed.

About a week later, when the landlord finally found out that we had six kids in the duplex, instead of the three my mother told him, he sent us packin. In fact, he came over to personally deliver the notice. He had a huge grin on his face while my mom begged to stay. But we kids could see she wasn't gettin anywhere. So Johnny and I went out to the landlord's car and paid it a visit. I watched as Johnny unzipped his fly and shot a stream of good ole Number One into the back seat of the landlord's new Caddy. That oughta do the trick, we figured. We walked back to the duplex when Johnny was emptied. From the front window, we watched as the landlord drove away, shakin his head to and fro when he finally noticed the smell.

It was time to move. Again. We only had a few days to get out. I barely had any time to tell suzy. She came to see me off on movin day. She was straddlin her pink, bannana-seat bicycle beside the gravel driveway leading to our duplex. She wore a white button-down shirt and a yellow skirt that gave her long legs room to breath in the Summer heat. suzy wasn't wearing her usual smile, though, and I couldn't help but wonder if she was sad because I was moving or because of IT.

My uncles had already moved all of the furniture so my mom loaded us kids up in the station wagon. We were moving back to the city, to a good ol' two-flat. Mom backed the wagon slowly down the driveway. As the car moved, I blew suzy a kiss and mouthed the words "I love you." I didn't say the actual words out loud cuz I didn't want my brothers to hear me. suzy caught my kiss and tucked it in her shirt pocket. Then she started to cry. She rode after our car, pedaling madly, as we turned out of the driveway, around the corner and over to the busy street. suzy screeched to a halt at Pulaski and watched as we made the final turn, her emerald eyes fixed on mine.

Holy Cross Hospital--Day 5

I ask if I can move over by the old guy. Tracie gives me the okay. She unplugs the tiny machine that sucks my blood through the tube and away I go. Tracie calls my machine, The Vampire. Makes sense to me. The old guy's napping and doesn't notice the move. It takes less than a minute. Thanks Tracie, I say and she says, Anything for you, Sweet Pea. That's what she calls me now, Sweet Pea. I don't mind that name. Tracie can call me anything she wants and I'd go for it. My buddies call me Folz. That's a nick-name offa my last name. Mr. Storch, the varsity basketball coach at my school, actually gave me that one. It's been like glue ever since. I'm on the sophomore team right now. But I practice with the varsity too. My school team is one of the state powerhouses. If I start when I'm on the varsity later, chances are I'll get a scholarship to college. Some of the guys on varsity have gone on to Iowa and Montana State and Washington State and North Carolina. I'm not that good. But I don't stink either. Free money to a nice little school down South would be just fine with me. Then, I could go huntin for my own little Tracie.

You'd get a kick outta my sophomore coach if you ever saw him. He's real skinny and has a face with white-as-death skin stretched tight across it. The dark hollows of his eyes seem to go on forever. He's a nice man. His name is Mr. Fegler. We call him Skull, but not to his face. All of us are in fear of the varsity coach. He's a yeller and a screamer and spit flies outta his mouth when he gets all worked up. And he don't even know it. I never saw a man get a face that red. One of these days he's just gonna pop like a too-tight, birthday balloon and that'll be the last we ever hear of him. None of the guys on my team fear our sophomore coach. Not a single one. But we all like him. Sometimes when he's drawing X's and O's on the chalkboard at half-time, one of my teammates will drop his shorts and flash his moon at Skull. He never sees it. He's too busy scribblin on that board. We just laugh. Bobby Malloy plays on the team with me. He's a decent hooper but he's much better at football. He's big and thick and has good hands. Definite tight end material. But I still like havin him on the hoop court. He rebounds like a bitch and if there's a loose ball near him, you better watch out if you're on the other team. Bobby will pancake you to get that ball. That's what I like about Bobby. He's got what the varsity coach calls "Killer Instinct." I got it too. I do anything to win--including playing dirty with punches to my opponent's gut when the ref's head is turned. Hey, why not?

The old guy just woke up. I allow him a minute to settle into the day and then I give him a hardy Hello. His eyes smile at me. I read him a few stories from the newspaper and he nods his head when I make insightful comments. I like this old guy. He's probably a pretty good grampa. I just wonder where his family is, though. Tracie says she talked to someone from the family once but that was days ago. I ask her to call again. She does, but she doesn't get anything but an answering machine. My whole family stops by to visit. It's good to see everyone. They can only come in to the ICU two at a time, so it takes a while to see 'em all. Wanda, the nurse who always works the shift after Tracie tells me the old geezer's name is Alcott, Taylor Alcott. I introduce everyone in my family to Mr. Taylor Alcott, and I let them know that he was a Ranger. Mr. Alcott can't say much. His throat and chest are all tore up. Tracie told me it's all from the smokes. Mr. Alcott's got throat and lung cancer and he's having a rough day getting any words out. When my family is all done visiting and long gone, Mr. Alcott takes off his mask and says, Thank You. It hurts him to speak and I can barely hear him, but I caught both syllables. I tell him he's welcome.

Brothers and Sisters

You already know my dad some. And you kinda met my mom, too. But let me tell ya a bit more about my brothers and sisters. Johnny's the oldest. He's got me beat by seven years. Then, there's Tim. He's just one year younger than Johnny. Jackie came one year after Tim. Then Mom and Dad took a four year break. That's when Sharon came along. I came one year after Sharon, and then there's Donna. She's the baby. She's three years younger than me and we're the only ones that have the crazy, Irish, flaming-red hair.

Johnny's nicest when he leaves us alone. But he's mean when he doesn't. He even seems like he's gettin meaner now that Dad isn't around as much. He always tells us that we stink or that we're stupid. He calls Jackie "Fatso" all the time and even sings his song for her. It goes like this. "Fatty, fatty, 2 by 4, couldn't fit through the bathroom door, so she sat and peed on the floor." Jackie cries when she hears that song, which is often. Johnny likes to throw the punches, too. That's okay, though. I can take it. Besides, one day, I know I'll get him back, and get him good.

Tim's a big guy. Strong as a bull. He's ten times tougher than Johnny, but he's tons nicer. He leaves me alone. He leaves most everyone alone. Mostly he just sits and watches and stays quiet. He's kinda like my grampa that way. You'll meet him later. Two years ago, Johnny and Timmy's 8th-grade basketball team won the city CYO championship for St. Sabina's and Timmy started every game the whole year even though he was only a seventh-grader at the time. Johnny was the leading scorer.

Jackie's kinda like a second mom. She watches over me, Donna, and Sharon, when Mom's at work. She is nice to us. I must confess that when Johnny sings his fatty 2-by-4 song, sometimes I join in. Jackie cries real hard then. And then I start feelin bad too.

Sharon's pretty tough for a girl. She can hold her own against me and I'm pretty tough, so I know she is too. She's good with her feet. She kicked me good in the marbles once. I went down quick and stayed there. Jackie came over to help. She pulled my shorts down and reached all around. Now I didn't like the idea of my oldest sister with her hands on my private marbles and all but something had to be done. I could barely breath and Mom was away as work. Turns out Sharon's foot pushed my marbles up and outta the sack--and into my stomach. Jackie pushed 'em back home where they belonged. I felt much better then, even though my marble sack turned different shades of black and blue. Those colors lasted for 'bout three weeks. Johnny made me show 'im my marble sack at night when we changed into our pajamas. He and Tim would point fingers at my sack and just bust up laughin. I'd chuckle then too.

Most little sisters are a pain in the rump. Donna sure is. She's always taggin around me and my friends. I tell her to beat it. When I get tired of her stickin around after I tell her to leave, I got no problem givin her a few punches. She leaves then. Once at home, I threw a pillow on Donna's head and gave her face a couple of flying knee drops, just like Dick the Bruiser on TV wrestling. When I pulled the pillow away, there was blood all over and Donna's front four choppers were layin on the floor like lost stones. I got in loads of trouble for that one. I deserved it, too.

Mom misses out on mosta this stuff. She's always at work. She has to be. Dad's either sick or working on gettin sick. He's not around much. When Mom's at home, we're good for her. We take it easy and let her rest. She needs it. I'm young but I know that without my mom, we wouldn't be a family. She's the glue that keeps us together. My dad wouldn't know what a tube of Elmer's looked like if his life depended on it.

Fire

I was deep into a fat sleep on a lazy Sunday morning at the new apartment at 64th and Kolin. Lazy, I say, cuz I knew we weren't gettin up early to go to Sunday mass. That much I knew with the utmost certainty. We seldom did the church thing anymore. Only the major holidays brought us to the altar. Mom worked late on Saturdays now and needed her snooze on Sunday mornings. There was no objection from us kids. So I could snooze the hours away until I shook from my slumber. In dreamland, I heard the words but didn't shake to right away.

"Wake up. Wake up." It was my brother Tim's voice. His lungs were piping the words out at full throttle, but in my state of sleep, his words were nothing more than a muddled whisper. "Fire. Fire." I didn't smell any smoke and I didn't feel any heat, but I started to come to. Bare feet pounded spastically about the hardwood floor of the apartment. I rolled to my side and stared down at my own feet. They were still warm under the covers. "Get up," Tim hollered. He was standing in the doorway of our bedroom. His eyes were stretched wide and his face was red and covered over with sweat. He was still in his pajamas.

I looked at Tim and then fell back into my bed. I wanted more sleep so I pulled the pillow over my head. But then Tim's hands were on my shoulders. And the pillow was gone.

"Fire! Get moving or you're gonna burn." Tim pulled me to my feet. A thin stream of smoke filtered into the room, its smell knifing through my nostrils. It looked like the long gray arm of a ghost at first, an arm that was ready to wrap itself around the bodies of stupid little boys like me. But then that arm grew muscles and filled up the entire room. I was fully awake now and I felt the heat at my feet.

"Where is she? Where is she?" It was my mother's voice, her searching voice, screeching from down the hallway.

I took off in a mad dash in search of that voice and ran smack into Donna as she came outta her room. She clanked to the ground. Her head put a little dent in the white hallway wall. Mom leaned over and helped me scoop Donna to her feet, but when Mom stood up, I couldn't hardly see her head. The gray smoke was everywhere now. All three of us ran towards the back door, hand in hand--with Mom in the lead. Tim was there waving us out onto the back porch. Within seconds, we were all down the porch stairs and we sprinted along the sidewalk to the alley. Everyone was there: Johnny, Tim, Jackie, Sharon, Donna, me, and Mom. Dad wasn't there, though. He missed all the fun. He was out of the sanitarium at the time, but still living on his own--the lucky guy. We all stood still as statues, statues with checkered and polka-dotted pajamas on, our eyes all aimed at what was fast becoming our former home. And as we stood there, I remember finding it strange that my feet were cold. Everything around us was hot, but yet my feet were cold. The fire tore away at the whole two-flat, at times its flames stretching tall into the sky like angry hands waving goodbye. And as I watched those flames wave, I wondered if they were cousins to the smoky hand that I first saw come into my room. And those flames changed colors, going from blue to yellow to orange and then back again. Non-stop circles of smoke climbed out of our apartment and that smoke turned the blue-white sky black. And as I looked at those clouds and those flames, I didn't think about my toys or my clothes, or my piggy bank containing my life's savings of $8.47. I just watched the flames and smoke and felt empty. It was the first time I ever felt that way and I didn't like the way it felt.

"The old ladies," Tim yelped. His eyes bugged and his chin was in his chest. He ran those eyes across all of us, searching for answers. I don't know what he saw in our faces, but Tim took off running.

"Don't," Mom yelled. "Stop." But Tim didn't stop. He raced to the back porch and shot up the stairs to the top flat. Two old ladies, the O'Neil sisters, lived in the apartment above us. We lived on the first floor and the owners, the Sheridans, were below in the basement apartment. Turns out, the Sheridans started the fire. After cooking up a nutritious bacon and eggs breakfast, they ran off to go to church with their bellies full. Problem was, they left the stove burner on and a greasy pan atop it. The grease caught fire and jumped and you can take it from there. While the Sheridans sang "Sons of God" at 8AM mass, their apartment building--with all of us nearly in it--was up in smoke.

We called the O'Neil sisters "Mrs. O'Neil" to their faces, but among ourselves they were simply, "the old ladies." Even my mom called them, "the old ladies." She was always sending us upstairs to bring "the old ladies" something or to borrow something from them. "Go upstairs to the old ladies for a couple of eggs," she'd say, or "The old ladies are back from the store. Go help 'em carry up their groceries." They were nice old ladies. Always. They were most generous with the dimes whenever we helped them with groceries, and they never frowned at us when we begged some goods from them.

The fire trucks still hadn't arrived as Tim scooted the last of the old ladies onto the porch. Flames jumped out the old ladies' bathroom window. Chunks of glass crackled and tumbled onto the cement gangway. Tim walked the old ladies as quickly as possible down the stairs, one on each side, both holding onto his muscular frame. When they made it to the bottom step, my mother raced over and helped lead them to the alley. They were both wearing matching pink housedresses with daisies climbing all over them. They stood with us in the alley and watched the fire eat everything that belonged to us. I turned my eyes towards Tim for a moment. Both of Tim's burly shoulders were kept busy by the heads of the old ladies.

"All of mother's photographs," the one old lady cried. "Gone, Martha. They're gone." Tears shook from her head.

"I know, Mary, I know," the other old lady said. Mary and Martha. That was the first time I heard their first names. They continued to glue their heads to my brother's shoulders and sob as the fire swept through the entire apartment. As I looked at the old ladies, it sunk in then what Tim had done. Without him, none of us would've made it. Some fireman probably would've found my skinny, little body layin in my bed, shriveled up like a piece of overcooked sausage. And this wasn't the first time Tim played the hero, either. When he was only ten, he saved Johnny from drowning in a Wisconsin Lake. So as I watched the flames that day, I found myself thinkin that I was lucky, lucky to have a brother like Tim. And that lucky feelin pushed that empty feeling I had earlier right outta my guts and into the sky with the clouds of smoke. I was proud to be in Tim's clan, proud to be a Foley. I had someone to brag about. Tim got us out of the fire and would never say a word about it. That's why I'm doing it for him.

Those hero-worshipping thoughts ended when I heard the screams of the fire trucks. Finally. Two trucks pulled in front of the house. Within minutes, water was spraying, windows were cracked open and firemen bounced around the remains of our flat. We cut through a neighbor's yard and walked to the front of the apartment. The street was filled with long-nosed neighbors pointing at the fire and at us. For the next hour, we watched the firemen work on the flames until there was nothing left but thin wisps of dying smoke. And when the fire was out, the firemen left and so did the long-nosed neighbors. It was just us and the O'Neil sisters out front, and all of us--except for Mom--sat on the curb.

"I'll be right back," Mom said. "I'm gonna go make a call." She started up the car with the extra key she always left under the mat and drove off. I knew what Mom was doin. She was drivin to a pay phone to call her dad--my grampa, Michael Roche. Mom was gone for just a few minutes. Grampa showed up twenty minutes later.

When he climbed outta his car with a load of blankets in his hands, he didn't say a single word--not a one. He simply wrapped the blankets over our frames and then walked to the sidewalk. Mom joined him. There, Mom talked for a few seconds, saying words I couldn't hear, and then Mom and Grampa walked into the apartment. They staggered through the mess. I could hear the occasional crinkling of broken glass or my mom saying, "No. I don't see it here." And I knew what Mom was looking for. No doubt, she went straight to her bed. The mattresses were burnt up though, and so was her tip money that she always kept in an envelope between those mattresses. She came back empty handed. I could see that from the look on her face. But that was Okay. We were pretty close to being broke most times anyway.

Grampa had an idea and I liked it too. "C'mon kids. Let's go to my place," he said. "We'll get ya good and warm and fill ya up with some of gramma's soup." The man spoke so sel-domly that I treasured every syllable. In those two sen-tences alone, Grampa said more than he'd said in two years. And it was a shame because his brogue was beautiful. Grampa Roche came from Templeglantine, County Limerick, Ireland. He took the boat to America in 1922 and that was all any of us knew about him at the time, including his wife. But later we would learn more.

We spent the next year living in my grandparents' one-bedroom apartment. It was quite a load. Six kids, two grand-parents and a mom. I'm sure those months were tough on my mom and on my grandparents too, but I never knew it. I was happy to be with them. At the end of the fourth month, Johnny, Timmy and Jackie left to live with Uncle Mike, my mom's brother. The so called little ones, that being, Sharon, Donna and me, stayed with Gramma and Grampa for almost another eight months. Mom bounced back and forth between us kids, sometimes sleeping with us and sometimes sleeping with the older ones.

Speaking of snooze, you shoulda seen my bed. I slept beneath the dining room table. Carpet over hardwood floor was my mattress and the mahogany table top, my canopy. Of all the places I have slept thereafter, none was ever so comfort-able. Heck, I was with Gramma and Grampa. You can keep those fancy hotels. This was as good as it gets.

Haircuts

The day following the fire, Grampa set up shop directly beneath the kitchen light, pulling a stool beside himself. With the precision of a surgeon, he arranged his barber's tools on the kitchen table. There were two different kinds of scissors, both with black handles. One was skinny and had long shiny, pointed blades, and the other had comb-likc teeth and was rounded atop. All the little attachable gizmos were there, too--the ones that snapped to the front of the clippers. Grampa laid them out in a straight line according to size. And then there was the clippers itself. I couldn't take my eyes off of it. It was ivory and black and shined like a brand-spankin new trophy. It was sittin right next to the pointy scissors. Just lookin at that clippers made me feel good cuz whenever it was on, it hummed away as it snipped off your locks.

We didn't really need haircuts that day, or so I thought. Grampa brought his traveling barbershop to our apartment two months ago, so our hair was still kinda short. But we didn't mind. Not one bit. Baldy Sours were the order of the day. Grampa never gave any other kind of cut. I went first. Such was the advantage of being the youngest. Johnny and Tim sat on kitchen chairs as Grampa readied himself to work his magic. They never considered leaving. Not on this day. Not on any haircut day. Grampa was a loving man who said little. We were all only too glad to sit and watch the man who spoke with his hands. And those hands moved gracefully, softly, soothing the fears that rumbled inside our scalps.

My father once took me to a barbershop. To me, it was a loud and ugly place, full of snarling-faced men who were full of both rude and silly comments. And when these men weren't yapping, their noses were stuck inside the pages of magazines and newspapers. Grampa's traveling barbershop was none of these things. He came to wherever we were living to give his haircuts, and these cuts were conducted in silence and most assuredly without the presence of mindless reading material. We would never consider reading while Grampa handed out his cuts. Never. On this day, Johnny and Tim waited happily in the near-silence, content to watch.

Grampa wrapped the shiny, green smock around my shoulders and pinned it snug to my neck. I looked up into his face. Unlike Dad, Grampa's face was a face that was always there when you needed it. Always. His face was wrinkled by time but still, to me, he wasn't an old man. He was so very, very alive. He wore black-rimmed glasses that took nothing away from his sea-green eyes, the eyes that held the mysteries of silence. The wide smile that always danced across his lips made him look even younger. Grampa then put his hands to me and his hands spoke. They said, "I love you, Dennis. I love you," and it felt so good to hear those words. He rubbed my neck and shoulders before working his fingers effortlessly across my ears, my nose, my temples. Then Grampa turned on the clippers and within seconds the clippers opened its mouth and hummed. Patches of my red hair spilled onto the smock. But then the hum grew softer. Grampa was standing in front of me. I leaned my forehead into his chest and I don't know what happened after that. I was out like a burnt out bulb, as usual. I could never stay awake during a cut. Never. None of us could. And we never tried to fight it either. My peaceful, energizing snooze ended that day when Johnny said, "C'mon squirt, you gonna sleep there all day, or what?" I snapped awake, ready to rumble. The green smock was gone, but Grampa's smile wasn't. He tapped me twice lightly across the top of my head and I jumped from the chair. That was his official signal that your haircut was over. I never left until I received my head tap.

Tim went next. Johnny and I watched Grampa work his magic on him. At the two minute mark, Tim was snoozin, and I mean out-cold snoozin. Grampa held the back of Tim's head when he had to, allowing it a gentle backward tilt as he worked the clippers with his right hand. When he was done, Tim's head was resting on Grampa's chest and his brown hair was clumped to the floor. Johnny's turn was no different. Tim and I sat in those kitchen chairs and decided to silently count how long Johnny lasted. I stopped countin at 100, not cuz I couldn't count higher, but because the counting took away from the watching. And guess what? Tim had Johnny's snooze button kickin in at 230 seconds. As usual, Grampa succeeded in putting all three of us under his peaceful spell, and as it turns out, we needed it--too. Grampa knew exactly what he was doing. The smell of smoke was no longer in my nose and the dancing flames were gone from my brain. And once the smock was offa Johnny, I raced my brothers to the bathroom where we fought for space to look at ourselves in the mirror. Always, after haircuts, we busied ourselves for several minutes gazing at our reflections, studying, admiring Grampa's creations.

Darts

The first time I saw old man Flynn I was 9 years old. That was in 1969, the same year the Cubs melted like a Hershey's kiss in the September sun and lost the pennant to the Miracle Mets. I was still livin with Gramma and Grampa back then. When Johnny, Timmy, and Jackie moved in with Uncle Mike, there wasn't a whole lot for me to do. Sure Donna and Sharon were with me, but I wanted a boy to play with. I got my wish when the Flynns bought the house directly next door to us. I watched the move from the back porch of Gramma's third-floor apartment. The sun beat down on the city that day, but my body stayed hidden in the shade that angled across the porch, so as not to be seen. And there was Mr. Flynn, standing in the middle of his tiny box of a back yard, the sun biting at his bare shoulders. His head stood tall and erect upon a thick neck that refused to bob whenever he moved. Even from twenty yards away, I could see that his face was cold and mean, cemented into a frown as he barked orders at his kids. From that distance, it looked like Mr. Flynn didn't have any eyes. He just had thin, black slits that were penciled in above his cheek bones. The kids showed no emotion when their father barked. They simply stared straight ahead, their faces blank as bathwater, as they continued to carry chairs, tables, books, toys, and clothes from the truck to their new home--moving all the while like soldiers marching in cadence.

I knew it wasn't polite to stare at others, but I couldn't stop myself. The Flynns had four boys and one girl, and one of the boys looked to be my age. I kept my eyes on him. The boy who caught my attention was a small fry with chicken-bone legs and stumpy arms. His tiny body made him look younger than he was, but his face told his true age and then some. Yep. He was a third-grader like me. During the move, he carried boxes twice his size but it didn't seem to slow him down any. I was most impressed. As I zoomed in on the back-and-forth activities of my soon-to-be new friend, I lost sight of Mr. Flynn. But then I heard his voice.

"Whataya lookin' at, ya nosy, little shit?" His brogue was thick and definitely Irish. Kinda like Gramma and Grampa's voice, only not nearly as nice. Mr. Flynn stood with hands on hips glaring up at me. I slid low beneath the banister, seeking protection behind the thick, gray slats.

"Stand up and show yerself," Mr. Flynn screeched. I peeked out between the slats. Mr. Flynn was in the same position, his slits still aimed at me. The Flynn kids kept on marchin to and fro without hesitation, their arms full. I crawled over to the screen door, cracked it open, and slipped inside--into the kitchen. Gramma and Grampa were there.

"What are ya doin', for crimminey sakes?" Gramma said. I was still on all fours. I raised my head. Gramma was standing at the stove, the tea kettle in her right hand, her eyes fixed on me. Grampa sat at the kitchen table, his face hidden behind the Sunday Sun Times. "What are ya doin?" Gramma said again.

"Ah, ah," I stammered, "just playin' army?"

"Army, huh?" She wagged her head in disbelief and set the kettle on the burner. "A likely story if ever there was one." Again she wagged her head. Grampa set the paper down and gave me a wide, knowing smile, a smile that said he too had been a boy once. I shot a stupid smile right back at him. He then grabbed the Comics section, snapped it open and again his face was gone. I sat on the chair directly across from Grampa, leaned over the tiny wooden table, and started reading the Comics part that was facing my way. That was the last I saw of Mr. Flynn for awhile and that was just fine with me. Cuz whenever I did see him, it never turned out good. But his son was another story altogether. I made fast friends with Michael Flynn. From the day following the move on, Michael and I spent most every day together. We played fast pitch at the school yard, Superball in the alley, and we even eyeballed some nudity magazines to expand our growing minds. There was no gettin to know each other stage. It quickly got so it seemed we could read each others thoughts. I knew if somethin' was botherin' him and he knew the same with me. There's no real way to explain it. That's just the truth. But the other truth was: no matter how hard we tried to avoid old man Flynn, he wasn't about to let that happen.

I was never formally introduced to Mr. Flynn. Michael was probably hopin I just wouldn't notice his father. That seemed to be his approach and that was fine by me. But how could you not notice that man? My first actual face to face with Mr. Flynn came about six weeks after the Flynns moved in. Michael and I were in his basement playing ping pong. I ran upstairs to take a squirt. As I hit the last stair and turned into the kitchen, my forehead banged smack into Mr. Flynn's chest. My eyes and ears were even with his heart. I saw no movement. I heard no pounding. Slowly, I let my eyes wander. He was the stuff carpenters were made of all right, thick-armed and barrel-chested. His face lacked all signs of warmth and life. I couldn't find a line or mark of any kind. And then I saw those eyes. Even from that distance, his eyes were still slits.

"What's dis?" he said, glaring at me. His few words brought the smell of gin into the room. I tried to answer but could only stutter."Who are you?"

"I . . . I--"

"Spit it out, boy," he said, his face fire-engine-red. I turned my eyes to the floor. Mr. Flynn shoved a muscular finger under my chin and raised my face until my eyes looked into his. Resting within the slits he had for eyes were slivers of the blackest pupils I'd ever seen. I was about to piss in my pants.

"Sean," Mrs. Flynn barked as she entered the kitchen. She examined us both and saw the fear in my eyes. "Leave the boy alone."

"Who's he belong to?"

"He's the Roche's grandson from the apartment," she said nodding her head toward my apartment next door. Mr. Flynn removed his finger and my chin fell to my chest.

"Aye," Mr. Flynn said, "the nosy one." He then made for the fridge in the pantry.

"Can I use the bathroom, Mrs. Flynn?"

Before she could answer, her husband spoke. "Tell 'im to use his own God damn bathroom. I don't need his piss on my floor."

"Shush, Sean," Mrs. Flynn said. She turned to me. "Go have your pee, Dennis. Pay him no mind. Have at the toilet and pee to your heart's content." I made it to the bathroom, barely, and shot my yellow stream into the water. I didn't have time to lift the seat, and even though I didn't get any drips on the seat, I still wiped it clean with toilet paper when I was done. I had a feeling Mr. Flynn would enter the bathroom after I left to make a thorough inspection. Once I flushed, I made it safely to the basement and I never used the Flynn bathroom again. Never.

But that was just the start of it. About six months after the move, bad things started happening all over the Flynn household. You see, Mrs. Flynn took a waitressing job. Now I couldn't blame her for wanting to get away from the old man, but with her gone, Mr. Flynn was at his worst. Not a single day passed where one of the kids didn't catch the buckle end of old man Flynn's belt. Mr. Flynn pinned Michael's oversized ears back more than a few times with me there watchin. He didn't care one bit that I was there. In fact, my being in the Flynn house seemed to inspire the old man even more. Now I've seen loads of parents whack or strap their kids when they felt their kids were outta line. But Mr. Flynn was all that and more. He made me thankful that my dad was the way he was. Sure my dad drank too much, but he almost never beat up on any of us. If I had to make a choice, I'd rather have a nonbeatin, drunk dad who wasn't around much than an always-around, drunk dad who liked to waylay his kids.

During one of my visits, I was playing Crazy 8's with Michael and his little brother, Hank. Mr. Flynn was out at the tavern and Mrs. Flynn was at work. No one else was home and Mr. Flynn wasn't due back til late in the evening. I planned to be long gone and in bed by then. We were at the kitchen table in the middle of a hand when Mr. Flynn came home early from the tavern. His new dogs, the ones he won in a card game, were with him. They were both Weimaraners. I couldn't say the name of that breed if you paid me. When the old man pushed his whiskey-red nose into the kitchen, Michael and Hank snapped to attention like enlisted marines at the sight of an officer.

"Where's yer mother?" he slurred. The stink from the corner tavern fell outta his mouth, heavier than his words.

Hank and Michael quickly eyed each other. "She's working, Dad," Michael said, shifting his eyes to his father. "She won't be home til--"

"I know. I know. I 'member now." Old man Flynn quickly ran his eyes around the room, until they rested on my face. He smiled.

"Whataya guys playin?"

"Crazy 8's, Dad," Michael said as he turned his head back to his cards. Old man Flynn slid over to Michael, grabbed him by the hairs at the back of his neck and pulled up.

"You lookit me when you talk ta me." He shook Michael's head from side to side. Hank turned away. The old man leaned in close to Michael's face. "Gottit?" Another burst of tavern-stink shot across the table.

"Yah Dad, I got it." Michael's eyes were fixed on his father. The old man released his grip. He ran his eyes across all of our faces. Then he snatched the cards offa the draw pile in the middle of the table.

"Hand 'em over," Mr. Flynn shouted. His palm was spread wide and flat in front of us. "C'mon. Cough up the rest." We all gave him the cards we held in our hands. Old man Flynn walked to the sink and tossed the cards atop the counter. He opened the fridge and pulled out a bottle of Old Style for himself. He cracked it open.

"Crazy 8's," the old man said as he wagged his head. "Dat's baby stuff." He took a swig of beer, muttered "baby stuff" again and then laughed for nearly a minute. I looked at Michael and then at Hank. They were both staring straight ahead, their eyes boring holes into the dull beige walls. When the laughter stopped, old man Flynn's face was beet red. "Get up," he screamed. "Now." Michael and Hank jumped to their feet. I wanted out of that place.

"Whataya doin, Dad?" Michael said.

"What am I doin? What am I doin?" The old man laughed and took another big swig of beer. "What kind of a stupit question is dat?" He raised his right arm and pointed to the pantry. "You know damn well what I'm doin." He jabbed his index finger again towards the pantry door. "I'm gettin the darts. It's dime game time."

Michael's head snapped my way. "You better get goin, Dennis." His words sounded like an order. I didn't know what was going on but Michael clearly didn't want me there, and that was just fine with me. I walked for the back door but stopped when old man Flynn stepped into my way.

"Don't leave Foley," Mr. Flynn ordered. He slurped the Old Style again and then grabbed my right arm. He walked me to the two-seater couch in the kitchen. The Flynns were the only family I ever saw that had a couch in their kitchen. "Sit right there, young Mr. Foley. Sit with Roscoe and Otto." Old man Flynn never called me by my first name and he had no desire to start now. I followed his command, dropping my butt upon the soiled, green couch, the royal Weimaraners serving as my bookends. I glanced at the hounds and found their faces offensive. Michael said those dogs went everywhere with his father but they wanted nothing to do with anyone else in the family. The hounds smiled, ready for the upcoming show.

Michael and Hank marched to their bedroom. Mr. Flynn eyed their tracks as he pranced back and forth in the kitchen, his tongue roaming across his smiling lips. For the first time, I noticed that everything about this man was sharp, deadly. His arms were skinny and stiletto-like and when he walked, those arms moved in a chopping motion. His legs were bony and long, almost devoid of muscle. Even old man Flynn's hair was sharp. His gray flat-top was home to millions of one-inch tall porcupined bristles patiently standing at attention.

The boys came out of their room with belts and pillows. Mr. Flynn spoke as Michael and Hank worked the belts and pillows into some weird kind of protection device, "You make it once, you get a dime. You make it twice, it's bonus time, 25-cents. You know the rules. Now, line up!" Mr. Flynn eyed me, that sinful grin still pasted to his face. And as he stared at me, that grin grew and grew. It was like he was saying, "Watch dis Foley. Watch dis. I'm doing this cuz you're here. Lucky you." My eyes wandered away and inspected the pale, blankness of the kitchen walls until I found the crucifix nailed above the rear door, the sole piece of decor in the kitchen. Even the savior couldn't bear to watch the upcoming show. His head dangled to the right, his eyes stared off into a lonely corner. The boys strapped the pillows across their backs with the assistance of each other, the belts holding the pillows in place as a shield. Their preparation was swift. This was a game in which they were well-practiced.

They walked to their father, stoically, focused on this odd game I knew nothing about. Mr. Flynn removed a handful of steel-tipped darts from the pantry. He walked to the center of the kitchen and halted at a foot-long scrap of electrical tape on the floor. I noticed the tape before. That scrap of tape was put there shortly after the Flynns moved in. I just never thought to ask what it was for. Mr. Flynn knelt behind the tape and stared down the shotgun hallway. The first door on the right was the old man's bedroom. Then came a bathroom on the left, followed by two more bedrooms on the right, and the living room at the front of the hall. As they marched into their father's room, Michael and Hank's freckled legs overflowed with energy. Old man Flynn squatted low, grasped one dart with his left hand and held the remainder in his right.

"You first, Hank," he commanded while stroking the darts. "You go when you're ready." I stiffened on the couch. The dogs sat proud and tall next to me, enjoying the view from their front row seats. Hank sprang from the door. The first turn out of the bedroom was difficult. He slid a bit, his socks failing to provide sufficient friction on the hardwood floor. Mr. Flynn flung a dart that struck six-year-old Hank in the right thigh. Hank screeched as the dart bounced off of him. Mr. Flynn flung another dart but missed high. He cursed himself. Hank ducked into the bathroom. Seconds later, he stormed from the bathroom and made his way towards the front room--bypassing the other rooms along the way. His father whipped a dart that hit Hank in the ass, but Hank said nothing as he fell into the frontroom. Then he turned around and walked slowly toward his father, tugging the dart out as he moved.

"You goin' again?" Mr. Flynn asked, glaring at his son. Hank said nothin. "I asked you a question. Answer it." Hank stayed mute. Mr. Flynn thwacked him across the face. "You goin again or not?"

"No, Dad."

"I didn't think so." Mr. Flynn wagged his head in disgust. "You're a pussy, Hank," the old man said, "and you're always gonna be a pussy." He tossed Hank's dime on the floor. Hank scraped up the dime and then took the stairs down to the basement. "You're up, Michael," old man Flynn screeched. I wanted to leave but was cemented with fear to the couch. But then the unthinkable happened. To my amazement, Michael completed this demented, homemade obstacle course without a scratch. He worked it smooth--zigzagging from room to room, until he reached the safety of the front room. Then he gathered up the stray darts and brought them to his father.

"Good aim, Dad," Michael said as he slapped the darts into the old man's outstretched hand.

Though he fought hard not to show it, Mr. Flynn was fuming. His nose reddened even more--and I thought that was impossible--and his ears transformed into miniature frying pans, ready to cook tiny eggs.

"No pain, no gain, Mr. Big Shot," Mr. Flynn snapped.

"No measly dime for me today, Dad," Michael bragged, "I want the big dough. I wanna go to the store, so I gotta buy my boy, Dennis, here a Twinkie too."

"You don't need to get me a Twinkie," I chirped.

"Shudup, Foley," Mr. Flynn commanded.

I fell back onto the couch with the smiling dogs, and as I looked at their faces, I wanted a handful of darts of my own to pluck out their eyes with. Michael pranced into his father's room with a gloating stride. He was enjoying his victory. Mr. Flynn stood up and dropped all of the darts but one to the floor. The discarded darts stuck in the wood floor like obedient slaves praying to their master. The old man remained motionless as Michael busted out of the first room like a bull raging through a just-raised, rodeo gate. Michael made it safely to the bathroom. There, he rested a moment. I knew what Michael was thinking. No more stops. Forget about the other bedrooms. He was going straight for the front room. Mr. Flynn musta read his son's mind, too. He smiled at me. Before Michael left the bathroom, Mr. Flynn worked a motion like a pitcher throwing from the stretch position. He lifted his right leg slightly, strode forward, and fired a strike just as Michael exited the bathroom. The dart hit its target. Michael crumpled to the floor and struggled like a wounded deer to right himself, his arms and legs flailing away at the empty hallway air. He made no sound; not even a whimper. He regained his balance quickly and sprinted for the safety of the front room. As he returned, he walked with a limp, favoring his right leg.

"I can't get it out," Michael said, tugging at the red dart. "I think it's in too far." When he removed his hand, I saw blood roll down his right leg, playing connect the dots with his freckles as it moved. The dart stuck out from his hip, the one-inch metal point fully buried in it.

"I'll get it for ya," Mr. Flynn said. He yanked out the dart with one swift, smiling pull. Michael said not a word, but tears of pain rumbled down his silky cheek. "You done good, Michael, real good. Here's your quarter." He slapped a quarter into Michael's hand. "Now wipe them damn tears from your eyes. God knows you aint no pussy."

We walked down the back porch steps and then Michael walked directly into the alley. Out of sight of his father, he leaned against his garage and slid down to the cement, right next to one of the garbage cans. He started to huff and puff deeply and he kept running both hands through his hair.

"You okay?" I asked.

"Yah. It hurts some, but I'm okay." Michael took a long, deep breath and released it. And as I watched him, all I could think of was boxing. Michael looked like a battered boxer, catching his breath on the canvass before rising, knowing there were many rounds yet to go. His stringy, blond locks covered his blue eyes. He wiped the blood from his leg with his right hand and ran that hand along his tattered, blue-jean cut-offs. I knew his leg was hurting, but his insides, his soul, were far more damaged. He finally wiped away his tears. "Just promise me, Dennis, promise that you won't say nothin' to no one, ever, O.K.?" I gave Michael my word, and--until now--my word I kept. But after Michael said that, he started puffing wildly for air, harder than even before, like he couldn't breath.

"Did I ever tell ya what happened to Finch?" he asked. Finch was the name of our pet cat. Michael and I found him one day and kept him hidden in the Flynn garage for six full months. Mr. Flynn rarely went into that garage, so we thought it was a safe place. We named that cat "Finch" after Atticus, Jeb and Scout from "To Kill A Mockingbird." My Grampa read that book to me and Michael that first Summer after Michael moved in, so when we found that cat—we knew the exact name we wanted to give it. And we played with Finch every darn day, until old man Flynn found out about him.

"No," I said softly. "You never told me." Then I looked directly into his eyes. "But I know."

"Do ya?"

"Yah." Michael looked at me and nodded his head. He knew I knew. He just didn't know how I knew. You see, the day I found Finch missing, Michael lied and told me that Finch must've run off. But I learned different. I had found Finch's bloodied body layin inside the Flynn garbage can when I was huntin for empty pop bottles. Even though Finch's eyes were spread wide open, I knew he was dead the second I saw him. Clumps of dried up blood were stuck to the fur around Finch's ears and mouth, and his stomach and chest were swelled up like a football. I closed Finch's eyes and left him there in that garbage can. A buncha time had come and gone since then and I still hadn't said a word about it to Michael. I guess I was waitin for him to say somethin to me. And now, he was.

"You wanna see 'im?" Michael asked.

"What?"

"Finch. You wanna see 'im?" I didn't answer. I just stood above Michael and eyeballed him. "I still got him."

"What?"

Michael climbed to his feet and pushed open the garage door. I followed him. He walked to the fridge and cracked open the freezer.

"C'mon and see him." He reached into the freezer and took out a large, folded-up brown paper bag. It looked like something a bunch of steaks or fish might be stored in. "He got me good that day he found out I been keepin Finch." Michael reached inside the brown bag and pulled out another folded-up brown bag. "He got my mom too. Beat her all up cuz she didn't tell him I had a cat." Michael pulled off one more layer of brown bag and there frozen and beautifully preserved was Finch. The tiger stripes that raced around his body were glossed over with frost. "He threw Finch back and forth against the walls of the garage till he was dead. Till he was dead!" I stared at Finch. A mound of frosty snow stood atop his head. His mouth was slightly ajar. I could see pieces of two of his teeth. "The stupid idiot don't know I keep him in here." He sat on the ground and set Finch on his lap like he used to do when Finch was very much alive. "He 's got old paintbrushes long frozen up and forgotten in that freezer. Stupid shit. He don't know what's in there." He ran his left hand across Finch's back. "And if he ever found 'im, I wouldn't care. I'd laugh my butt off. I know it'd scare the crap outta him." A rebel's grin was cemented to Michael's face.

I walked over for a closer look at Finch.

"Go ahead and pet 'im if you like." I didn't. Michael continued to pet Finch's frozen body. "I take him out sometimes and talk to im, pet im." I stayed quiet, very very quiet. "You sure you don't wanna pet im." I shook my head in the negative. And then I thought back to my dad and the O'Neil's cat, Mike. And I wondered why all cats turned up dead when I was was around. And then my brain clicked.

"I think we should bury him," I finally said. It seemed a reasonable thing to do.

"Why?"

"I dunno. I just do."

"That aint good enough."

I thought fast. "We need to bury him so he can go to heaven. Dead things need to be buried so they can go."

Michael balled his face up and swung his head from side to side. "My dad aint goin to heaven when he dies."

"I know. But Finch wasn't nothin but good. He's for sure goin to heaven. So let's let him go."

Michael didn't say anything. He tucked Finch neatly back in the layers of brown bag and placed him back in the freezer. He closed the freezer door with a bang and stared at me with his father's stare. I stared a mean stare right back, thinking about the icy cap atop Finch's head and his new paper bag home. But I said nothin.

Holy Cross Hospital--Day 6

When I woke up this morning, Mr. Alcott's head was twisted my way and he was starin at me with his eyes spread wide. Morning, Mr. Alcott, I said with a wave. He nodded his head and kept up with that starin. But I didn't mind it. Like I already told ya, old Mr. Alcott's a nice man. He wasn't workin those eyes over me like I did anything wrong. He was just kinda starin and noddin his head. Maybe he was tryin to sort out how I ended up in this dump of a hospital. Or maybe he's just thinkin about other things and usin my body as a sponge for his thoughts. You ever try that? I sure do. Sometimes if I stare a hole into the paneled wall of my bedroom at home--while I'm tryin to figure somethin out--the answer just seems to come to me. The same thing happens at school. My geometry class is in a room that's directly across the courtyard from the Dean of Discipline's room. Old Brother Donlon, the dean, is one rough monkey. Sometimes I catch him beltin some kid around in there. He's cracked me across the noggin with that big ring on his right hand before, too. But sometimes, when I'm tryin to work through different angles and geometry calculations, I just stare across the courtyard. Most times, Bro Donlon's suckin on a mug of coffee, and as I watch him slurp that coffee, the answers seem to float my way. I can't explain it. Just staring at him and that cup, or at the wall at home, helps me focus, I guess. Maybe that's what old Mr. Alcott was doin. So stare away. It's A-okay with me. I don't mind bein a sponge for Mr. Alcott.

Tracie bops into the room all full of smiles. So my little Sweet Pea's finally awake, huh? she says. She checks her watch. It's 9:30, she says. You got at least 10 hours worth. I laugh and nod my head. Tracie brings Mr. Alcott and me our breakfast. She sets my tray on one of those adjustable food tables, and then wheels that table over to me. She swings the table into place--right over my lap--and then lowers it by pressing the lever on the side. I get a kick outta that table. Whoever came up with that idea musta made a buncha money. Who knows? Maybe that person made it at first to care for some sick relative who couldn't get outta bed, someone like Mr. Alcott. I pull the plastic cover offa my breakfast plate. A gush of steam floats up into my face. And there's my breakfast, watery scrambled eggs, toast, and two sausage links that look like burnt fingers. Not exactly like how Mom does it, but it'll do. I wolf mine down, but Mr. Alcott doesn't touch his. He hasn't had much of anything to eat the last few days. He does slide his mask off, though, to drink his orange juice.

Tracie comes back a little later to clear out our trays. The smile on her face leaves when she looks at Mr. Alcott. Her eyebrows shoot up too. I turn to my right. Mr. Alcott's waving Tracie to his bed. She moves in and leans over him. Mr. Alcott takes that mask off and talks in whispers into Tracie's ear. When he's done, Tracie stands tall and slips her hands down to her hips. Her elbows stick out like chicken wings. You think so, huh, Mr. Alcott? Tracie says. You think Sweet Pea might be good at it? Mr. Alcott nods his head. His mask is back in place, but I can see a wide smile inside that mask. I don't quite know what's going on, so I keep my mouth zippered shut. That's always the safest way.

I'll be right back, Tracie says. She leaves the room with our breakfast trays in hand and comes back a few minutes later. She's carryin some blank sheets of paper in her hand and a pen between her teeth. She rolls my food table in between my bed and Mr. Alcott's bed. It's a snug fit. Tracie sets the paper and pen on the food table. Mr. Alcott invites you to play Tic-Tac-Toe with him, Tracie says. I look over at Mr. Alcott. He nods his head. Sounds good to me, I say. I'll play. Tracie pulls the lever on the food table until the table top hits the perfect height. She lowers the top half of Mr. Alcott's bed just a bit. My bed is bent just fine so Tracie leaves mine alone. Mr. Alcott reaches out with his long, bony right arm and grabs the pen. His tattoo is staring me in the face. How do ya like Mr. Alcott's tattoo, I say to Tracie. He was a Ranger. Yes, he was, says Tracie. And now he's a keeper, Tracie adds, a real keeper. She pats Mr. Alcott on the shoulder. Mr. Alcott wags his head and releases a tiny grin. He uses his pen to mark the four lines that make up our game and leaves his hand rest on the table. The lines are surprisingly straight and crisp. He's probably taken a drafting class or two in his day. Tracie grabs a chair and watches. Mr. Alcott takes the X's and I take the O's. He beats me up good for four straight games--even when he let me go first. I win the next one though, and then we hit a Cats game on the sixth game. Tracie slipped out right about then. I didn't actually see her go. I just caught a piece of her pink smock floatin out the door.

I've always liked Tic-Tac-Toe. It's probably the only game I can ever really remember playin with my dad. We used to play at the kitchen table when I was a first-grader over at our Throop Street apartment. It's a thinkin man's game, my dad would always say as he put the lines to the paper. Then he'd tap his head and say, yep, a thinkin man's game. I play Mr. Alcott for about an hour and a half straight. He takes about two outta every three games. He doesn't let me win on purpose either--like I'm some little kid--and I like that. We pass the pen back and forth after each X or O, his old, wrinkled fingers meeting my young, freckled fingers each time in the middle of the table.

The Roach Motel

After a year at Gramma's, Mom moved us to a new apartment outta the city, close to Mom's new waitressing job—at The Barn, in a suburb called Burbank. Mom said Dad was doin loads better and he was coming to live with us, too. The older ones were coming back from Uncle Mike's and we were all going to be a family again. I didn't want to leave Gramma and Grampa or Michael, but since we were all going to be together again, I thought it was worth a shot. Besides, Gramma and Grampa weren't goin anywhere. I'd see them and Michael whenever I came to visit. The excitement over the move wore off after just a few weeks. That's when Mom sent Dad packin. He was all about the drink again, going to the taverns sprinkled along 79th Street and draggin me with him. I knew then why my brothers stopped going with Dad years ago. I was tired of watchin him down beer after beer and whiskey after whiskey. Sure all the taverns we went to had games and pin-ball machines, but I no longer felt like playin them. When Mom kicked him out, Dad rented a place close to the horse track where he still worked.

Our new apartment building was stacked atop a laundromat, and there were two other apartments directly next to us--with all of us on the same floor. The building itself was made of solid, red bricks, but the guts of the apartment were anything but solid. The walls were paper thin and you could hear most everything going on in the apartment next door. I quickly learned to like the new place, even though there was little reason to do so. Johnny took to callin it the Roach Motel and he was right. The laundromat below us was infested with cockroaches and seeing how they were somewhat adventurous creatures, they liked to explore--which meant that they climbed the walls up to our apartment and we too were infested.

When you opened the kitchen cabinet to get a glass or plate, whole armies of the critters scattered like buckshot before your eyes. Mom made us wash every glass or plate we took from the cabinet. She was smart. It was a good habit to get into and all of us developed the habit. You had to. If you didn't, you might find a cockroach giving a speech in your glass of milk.

"Wash off those footprints," Mom would say when we pulled out a glass, referring to the cockroach prints. We lived above the laundromat for four years. That was our longest stint ever in any one spot. Though Dad was rarely with us, we were never without the roaches. Those lovely bugs had such big hearts too. They always wanted to keep you company, no matter where you went. At times, while I sat in class at school, I'd find a roach slipping out of my shirt sleeve to say hello. I'd smush 'em before anyone saw it, or at least I hoped I got him before anyone saw him. When I told Mom about the roaches' school visits, she told all of us to make certain we gave our clothes a good shakin before putting them on. So we did. But it was clear to all of us that our apartment was more their home than ours. We waged war on occasion, tossing exploding bug killing bombs into the apartment and then returning later in the day to find the apartment filled with so many dead roaches, the wooden floor looked like one huge, bumpy brown carpet. But the roaches were never gone. They just wouldn't die off. Finally, we just resolved to live in semi-peaceful co-existence with them.

All in all, though, I liked the new apartment. I painted a strike box on the side of the apartment wall and played fast-pitch nearly every sun-shiny day. Mosta the time I played fast-pitch with Harry. He was my new best friend. He lived across the alley from me in a tiny white house that all the kids in the neighborhood called, the Igloo. Harry had a big ring around his belly, just like the planet, and his hair was as black as a witch's hat. He didn't have a dad either cuz he died when Harry was just a baby. If we weren't playing baseball, Harry and me were inside the laundromat. It was one of those places without a person there to watch you. All of the machines were automatic, operated by coins. I'll tell you right now that sometimes I stole from that laundromat. I could fit my bony arm all the way up into the Pepsi machine and pull out pops for everyone. Sometimes we'd toss a dime into the jumbo dryer and take rides. That was one of Harry's favorite games. We'd put a dime in the slot, Harry would jump in, I'd press the GO button, and there went Harry spinning about and screeching away, yelling "Yee-ha" like he was ridin the Cisco Kid's horse. But dimes were hard to come by so we didn't play that game too much. Instead, we spent most of our time walking in circles in the laundromat and stompin on every roach we found.

The Sanitarium

Mom is taking me, Sharon and Donna with her to the sanitarium to see Dad. Only problem is Mom's not letting us come inside to see him, once we get there. "Little kids aren't allowed in the sanitarium," Mom told us back at the apartment. We're coming with on the ride cuz none of the older kids can watch us today. They're all busy. I don't know why we can't just watch our own selves. We do it most times during the week already. But Mom's funny about her days off. If she has to go somewhere, she always takes us with her if one of the older ones can't watch us. Sharon's sitting in the front seat next to Mom. I usually snatch that seat when it's just the three of us, but Sharon beat me to it today. That means I get to sit in the back seat with Donna. Such joy!

You hit a lot of lights and stop signs when you head up to the far Northside. And you pass a bunch of L trains too. The Northside is far away from where we live. You pass by all the Southside streets with the numbers on 'em--like 71st Street and 63rd Street and 35th Street, and you know you hit the Northside when the streets don't have numbers anymore--just names, names like Division and Armitage and Fullerton. There's all sorts of angled streets too. Gramma Roche says it was an Irishman who laid out the plans for the streets in Chicago, but he planned-out the Northside streets after a night of too many Guinnesses. We pass Riverview Amusement Park on the way. It's closed now, but you can still see lots of the rides reaching up into the clouds like skyscrapers. Mom took us there twice that I remember, when it was open. I went on some of the rides but stayed offa most--like the parachute and the Bobs. Some kids got hurt and died when the Bobs sailed right off its roller coaster track one day. I think that's why they had to shut down. I like the face on the guy at the front of the park. It's at least twenty feet tall. He looks like some kind of a wild gypsy with his handkerchiefed head and gold earring. He's looking at me as we pass him by. I give him a wink but he doesn't wink back.

Mom is listening to the radio as she drives. She and Sharon hum along with some of the songs. But I don't care about that radio. I'm thinkin about Dad as we drive. I wonder why kids can't go inside the sanitarium. And just what is a sanitarium anyway? I know it's like a hospital, but different too. Dad's been there a bunch, but I still don't know what it is exactly or what it's like. I wanna go inside to see for myself and I wanna see Dad. I wanna tell Dad that I hope he feels better soon. I bet Sharon and Donna are feelin the same way. I think some more and then I decide it's time to talk.

"How come kids can't go in the sanitarium, Mom?"

"It's just a rule, honey," Mom says. "Just one of their many rules." Mom turns the dial on the radio and Sly & the Family Stone starts in about Everyday People. "I'll only be in there for a few minutes anyways. Dad just has to sign some forms and then I'll be right back."

"What kind of forms?" Sharon asks.

"Just forms, forms for school. You know, so, so we can get a break on the tuition."

Donna is making beeping sounds next to me. I watch her for a second to see just what she's up to. She can be a real pain on car rides. Most times she cries about being car sick and if she's not doing that, she's kickin at ya with her bony legs. Like I got nothin better to do than sit in a car and get kicked by my little sister. But today she's minding her own business and just beeping. It doesn't take long to figure it out. She beeps every time she sees a semi-truck pass by. I like doing that when you see a Volkswagen Beetle--cuz you really have to pay close attention to the road to find them--but there's way too many semis around. Lame game, I decide, so I don't join in. I listen to Sly.

There is a blue one who can't accept the green one
For living with a fat one trying to be a skinny one
And different strokes for different folks
And so on and so on and scooby dooby doo-bee
Oh sha sha--we got to live together.

"Ok guys, just a few more blocks," Mom says. She turns the radio off. We are on Pulaski now--that's a street that goes all the way to my neighborhood too--and when I look up, we pass a stop light street with the name "Foster" on it. I never heard of that street before.

"I'm hungry," Donna says. I'm hungry, too, but I don't say so.

"Ok," Mom says. "That's what we'll do." Mom smiles. "After I see your dad, we'll get a snack. On the way back, okay?"

"Yee-hah," Donna says. Sharon and I both nod our heads. We like going for snacks with Mom. Every month, Mom will start one day late at work just so she can pick us kids up at school for lunch. We usually go to McDonalds. I like that place alright. When Mom knows she has to work late, she leaves us little ones a dollar each for dinner. We always walk over to Henry's at 79th and Narraganset, in Burbank, with our three dollars. For $1.00 even--95 cents plus tax--you can get a hamburger, a hot dog that comes with a small fry wrapped up with the dog, and a pop. We love Henry's. We go there at least two or three times a week. I really don't care where we eat today. All I know is I'll be ready.

Mom hits the right turn signal and slows down. We turn into a road that has a guard shack just inside it. There's a sign out front but I missed it cuz I was looking for the guard in the shack. No one's standing guard so Mom drives slowly past the shack. She crawls along a narrow bending road. This place reminds me of a cemetery with all the curvy roads, cept this place has huge brown brick buildings with tile roofs all along the road instead of grave stones. All of the buildings look like they could be twins, and all stand three stories tall. The only thing that makes them look different is they all face in different directions, all tilted a little one way or the other.

Mom drives the road past all the houses and never once looks up. Her eyes are fixed on the curves and bends in the road. And then suddenly, she stops. She parks the car in front of the second to last building. She grabs her purse and jumps out of the car. Then she sticks her head in through the open door.

"I'll be right out. Just count to 500 and I'll be out. Okay?" We nod our heads.

I stare up at the brown brick building in front of us. This sanitarium looks very much like a hospital but a sad hospital at that. I don't know why I feel that way but I do. All of the hospitals by me--Christ Hospital and Holy Cross and Little Company of Mary--are right out in the open on the busy streets where everyone can see 'em. This place is covered up by all the tall trees around here, tree after tree after tree. If you drove past this place on the busy street, you'd never see it. It's like someone's trying to hide this place away where no one can find it. In my school, there is a boy in my class who has a retarded little brother and you almost never see him. I think the parents are ashamed of him, and that makes me mad. He can't help it the way he is. He didn't do anything. I wonder if they keep him locked up in the basement. This place gives me the same kinda feeling and I don't like the idea of my dad being here much at all. But then I see a head move inside a window. This building is loaded with windows. Most of the windows are covered over with gray blinds, but then again--they could be white blinds that just have lotsa dust on 'em. I look into the uncovered windows to see if, maybe, Dad is sittin in the window lookin out at us. I don't see him in any of the windows, including the one where I thought I saw a head move. I wonder what the inside of this building looks like. My mind starts to wander.

I am in the hallway now on the third floor, searching for Dad's room. The hallway is long and skinny like the road we just drove down, cept it straight and not curvy. The hallway is kinda dark. Most of the hallway bulbs are out or just plain don't work. Either way, someone needs to call a good electrician. I walk and walk down this long hallway, stepping upon square after square of dark brown tile floor. This place smells like a hospital, but only worse. The smell is kinda like the smell of the old folk's home where Gramma Foley lives. I been there before. Lotsa times. There are nurses in this place, posted like guards every fifty feet or so, but none of them have any teeth--or at least they don't show 'em. The nurses in the hospitals by me smile when they see a young kid like me. Not these nurses. They keep their mouths closed tight. I know that this is not a happy place. I know that now with utter certainty. I turn at the corner of the long hallway and walk a bit more. Then I see Dad's name scratched across a piece of white tape that's stuck to a solid wooden door. The tape says "J. Foley." I put my hand on the door knob and twist. I start to push the door open, ready to see Dad's face. Instead, the car door flies open and Mom climbs inside.

"See. That wasn't so bad, was it?" she says.

"I counted to 850," Sharon says.

"Me too," Donna says.

"You can't count past 20," Sharon says. I'm glad she's not lettin our little beast of a sister get away with that.

"Can to," Donna says.

"Cannot," Sharon says.

"Okay, okay, already," Mom shouts to stop all the cannot-in and can-to-in. "Stop the fighting and we'll go get that snack I promised ya." We all get quiet. Mom starts the car and turns it around. She makes her way down that winding road again.

"How's Dad doin?" I ask.

"He's getting better," Mom says quickly. She turns the wheel and glides around a curve in the road. "He said to say hello to the three of you." We glide past a few more bends in the road and pass the guard shack. I turn back and stare out the window at the sign I missed when Mom drove in. I read the letters on the sign but I have never seen one of the words before. I try to sound the word out, out loud. "Tub"--"Tube"--"Tub-er-lo—"

Sharon turns around and says, "That's 'Tuberculosis', you big dummy." Sharon does okay in school but she's not as smart as she thinks she is. I stick out my tongue and shake it at her. She turns back the way she should be.

I wanna ask Mom what that word means, but I don't. Sharon said it nice and fast and it sounded good. I know I couldn't pronounce that word, not for a million dollars. But still, what does it mean? I wanna know. I decide to ask, even if it I can't say the word right and sound stupid.

"What's Tuby-closis?" I say. The word came out fast. It didn't sound as good as when Sharon said it, but it was better than I thought I'd say it. Sharon twists around again and looks at me, but then she spots her eyes on Mom.

"Tuberculosis is a disease," Mom says. Her words come slow. "It's what your father has, right now. That and some other things."

"Will he die, Mom?" Sharon asks.

"I don't think so, honey." Mom stares into traffic as she talks. "He needs to take better care of himself, though, when he gets out."

"Look," Donna screeches. “McDonalds.” Mom quickly turns right and pulls into the McDonald's parking lot. We go inside to order the food, and then take it back to the car and eat. We sit in the parking lot and munch, but now the food tastes different. Very, very different. And I'm not so hungry anymore.

Father Mac

Harry went to the public school and I went to the Catholic school with Donna and Sharon. The school let us go for free on account of the fact that Mom didn't have the money for tuition. But I didn't go to the Catholic school for long. Father MacMahon called me to his office. He was the associate pastor at St. Colleta's, and the school principal.

"We need to have a discussion, Dennis, and I believe you know what it's about." I knew all right. I beat the snot out of two kids. They deserved it.

"Yes, Father," I said.

"I want your father here with you."

"Can't my Mom come instead?"

"I'm afraid not, lad. This is a discussion about fighting and I believe your father should be the one I talk to." He saw my long face. "Is there some problem?" He was genuinely concerned. He didn't know the situation. I didn't have the heart to tell Father Mac that my father wasn't around much anymore. Mom still had my dad listed on the school info sheets, just like he was livin at the Roach Motel with us. Only he wasn't. Since Mom kicked Dad out two years ago, I saw him about three times. He looked worse each time I saw him. He'd been in and out of sanitariums and hospitals still getting his ulcers and stomach and lungs and other parts worked on. All of us kids had to go get TB (that's short for tuberculosis and much easier to say) shots cuz Dad still had that disease when he came by to visit, once. Shots. I hate needles. To make it up to me and the others, Dad sent little trinkets to us each of the last two Christmases. He sent me two glasses he personally made. They let him do crafty kinda stuff like that in those hospitals and sanitariums, I guess. Mom said the glasses weren't really glasses. She said they were German beer steins. All I know is

I liked 'em. They had painted pictures of little guys with funny, feathered hats on 'em, and they had tops to 'em that opened up and stayed attached by way of the hinges. I haven't seen either of my steins lately, though. I think my brothers put them to use on the weekends.

"No, Father," I lied, "there's no problem. When do ya wanna see my father?"

"When do you think he can be here?"

"Well, he gets offa work about 4:30 and comes home and eats."

"Do you think 7:00 should be good?"

"Yes, Father."

"Ok then. Let's make it Wednesday at 7:00 in my office. If there's a problem with that you let me know." I told him I would. "And let's have no further problems with you either." I nodded. I liked Father MacMahon. He wasn't a young man but he seemed young cuz he wasn't mean and ogre-ish like Father Hogan, the pastor at St. Colleta's. And, unlike most priests, Father Mac didn't even have a rump-whacking paddle for use on the bad kids. I was extremely thankful for that.

I told my mom about the appointment. She contacted my father. He said he'd be there.

"Do you think he'll come, Ma?" I looked for an answer. Mom was silent. "He's the one who said it was okay. He said he'd come if I got into trouble."

My mother searched for pain in my face. "I really don't know, Honey. I know he said he'd come if you got in trouble. I only hope he does." She grabbed my arm and pulled me to her lap. "If he doesn't come, you tell Father Mac that I'll meet with him on any Monday or Tuesday night. Those are the only two nights, though."

"I know, Mom." She waitressed on the other nights.

I waited for my father in Father Mac's office that Wednesday, hoping he was on his way. Father Mac was in another room. Framed certificates from several colleges that had fancy writing all over 'em, and a shiny, gold, foot-long crucifix clung to the wall behind the priest's desk. There were no photographs or other indications of life on the wall. The priest's huge desk was bare except for a bible that looked like it had been beaten-up by time, and two ink pens that someone probably gave Father Mac as a present--tilted like canons in their golden holders. I liked Father Mac. He was fair and good to me, but I could do without his office. It gave me a chill and made me think of dead bodies layin in the county morgue waiting to be claimed.

At 7:11, my father waltzed through Father Mac's door. He was without the smell of beer or whiskey. I was happy. I smiled at him and then I saw how old and haggard he looked. It had been eight months since I last saw him. He put on ten years during that time.

Father Mac entered his office from an adjoining door. My dad shook the priest's hand, and immediately summoned me to his side. I sat promptly in a wooden chair as directed by my father. He took off his dark brown fedora and held it tightly with both bony hands. After Father Mac sat down, my dad settled into his chair.

Father Mac stared across his desk at us. He smiled and spoke slowly.

"I told Dennis not to fight, Mr. Foley."

"I see," my father stated.

"I told him that fighting is the work of the devil. Nothing good comes of it."

"I see."

"He seems to understand what I've told him and I hope there will be no more fighting."

"I see," my father said again. He removed his right hand from his fedora and ran it slowly through his full head of hair. For a moment, my father stared at the paint chips on the plaster ceiling, working on his thoughts. He finally looked at me and smiled. "Do you understand what the Father's tellin you, Dennis?" Dad asked.

"I do," I answered.

"You know exactly what he means?"

"I do."

"And do you agree with it, son?"

"No, Sir," I announced as proudly as a Marine recruit. The eyeglasses Father Mac held in his hands clanked upon his desk. Rarely was his precious advice turned away from him, at least not before his very eyes.

"What's this you're saying?" the priest asked.

"He said he doesn't agree with ya, Father," my dad said.

"Well, that's why you're here, Mr. Foley, to straighten him out."

"I'm afraid I can't do that," my dad said rather matter-of-factly. "In fact, I won't do it."

"Well then, Mr. Foley, you're teaching Denny here that violence is good, that violence is the answer."

"Not necessarily, Father."

"I don't get it," said the flustered priest. He wrapped his hands together in a prayerful position, resting his chin upon the tips of both thumbs. "What . . . what are--"

"I'm the one that told him it was okay to take whatever measures were necessary to keep those two derelicts off his back. My wife and my son told me how these kids had been after him since he moved in. It's tough coming to a new place, Father. We've moved a bunch and he's always having to deal with crap like this." My dad worked his eyes into the ceiling again before turning back. "See Father, Dennis is a good kid, a smart kid. Maybe it doesn't show all the time, but he is. I know he's fidgety, and he stutters, and he has a hard time staying still, but he's smart. I know it. It's locked up somewhere inside of him, looking for a way to get out. He doesn't deserve those punks chewin after him all the time. Teasin him about his stutterin. Teasin him about havin to wear the Dunce hat. So I told him he could kick their ass and not worry about gettin in trouble about it, 'cuz I said I'd back him up."

"But he nearly caved in young McNally's head with that bat and he punted Ralston so hard in the groin, his balls look like they belong in a bowling lane."

"So be it, Father. They won't mess with 'im anymore."

"You're teaching him wrong, Mr. Foley," Father Mac screeched, aiming his Christian finger across the desk like a gun.

Dad jumped from his chair and tossed his fedora on the seat. "Shit Father, I'm teachin my son to win. He's learnin to take care of himself, to survive." He paced the hard-wood floor for a moment. When he stopped, he stared at Father Mac and slowly released a crooked smile.

"You're a good man, Father. I don't know you but that's what everyone keeps tellin me. But, you got it nice here. Real nice. Maybe you don't see it the way I see it, but the world aint always such a wonderful place. And quite frankly, I don't think it's gonna get much nicer any time soon." Again my dad paced the hardwood floor, speaking as he moved. "So if I can leave my kids with anything--anything at all, it's about winning, it's about surviving." He blew out a big sigh. "See Father, I don't want Dennis to end up like me." My dad stopped pacing. He stooped down, set both of his hands on the priest's desk, and leaned forward. "I may not be much of a father, but I know what I know and I'm not afraid to say it. The Southside is full of Irish drunks and I'm one of 'em. It can do without one more. I want something more for my son. No one's gonna keep him down, certainly not a couple of punks. The next generation gets what the prior generation couldn't even see. That, in my opinion, is what life is all about, Father." The priest glared at my father until his glare became a wordless, empty gaze. My dad stared back, considering the priest's expression. He then donned his hat, grabbed me by the hand and pulled me towards the door.

"Let's go, Dennis," Dad said as he looked back at the priest from the doorway, "Nothing more need be said here." I gladly held on to my father's bony hand. I was proud to be a Foley, proud to have my dad as my father. He was there for me like he said he would be and he backed me like he said he would. Not only that, but he got the last word in on a priest, leaving him speechless, and that was a top-notch feat in and of itself. The Corvair was waiting outside the rectory. Dad drove me back to the apartment. I spoon-fed him the latest news during the ride before he curbed the car outside the apartment. He turned to me and stared deeply into my eyes, like he knew what the future held.

"Be good, Dennis. Be good and try hard." He stopped and rubbed his bony fingers along his thighs. "That's about all I can tell ya. And try not to ever give up. Ever." I didn't quite know what my dad was trying to tell me at the time. Maybe he knew that his final days on earth were slipping away. I didn't. He forced a smile. "Get going or your mother'll send out a search party for ya."

"Thanks, Dad." I jumped from the car and watched him drive out of sight. That was the only time my father ever spoke of his expectations for me, and the only time I heard him openly admit that he was one with the Irish curse. When I laid down that night, I couldn't sleep. I had far too much to think about.

Dad's Place

My dad stayed out late last night. I heard him stumble in. He's still not livin at the Roach Motel with us, but Mom lets him stay, sometimes. He slept on the front room couch. Least that's where I found him this morning. I woke him up. Man oh man did he have a case of bad breath. There's nothin worse than day-old, whiskey breath. But we're in the car now. Mom's drivin Dad back to his place. He rents a room across the street from Sportsman's horse track, where he works. As his job, he's still one of them guys who stands behind the window with jail bars on it and takes your money and bets. Mom drives a 1965 Ford Galaxie that Grampa gave to us. It's two-tone blue. It's not supposed to be two-tone, but it is cuz Earl Scheib didn't do a good job matchin the colors after Mom had an accident.

Mom and Dad aren't talkin as she drives. I'm sittin behind my dad and Donna is sittin behind my mom. Mom keeps turnin her head and lookin at Dad, but he doesn't even notice her eyes. He just stares out the passenger window like there's mounds of gold layin on the side of the road. We stop at a red light at 63rd and Cicero. A CTA bus pulls alongside us. My mother eyeballs it.

"Why couldn't you just take the bus?" she says.

"I didn't think you'd mind driving me over to—"

"Is that right!" Mom says. My dad is lookin at her now. Her eyebrows are pointin almost straight up.

"Well," my dad says apologetically, "I didn't think—"

"That's half your problem. You didn't think. You never think." She squeezes her eyes till the lids are almost shut. "The other half is you never do. Never do. You never, ever, ever do." My dad drags his cigarette and points his eyes back out the passenger window. This is very unlike my mom. She almost never has these types of "chats," as she calls em, with us kids around. But she's not as smiley anymore. That's the one thing I notice most about her. Even without my dad around, she don't smile much anymore. Not even when I try my best jokes on her.

I look over at my sister. She has my GI Joe in her left hand and her Barbie doll in her right. I didn't bring Joe. Either she brought him without askin or I left him in the car before. Joe and Barbie have their arms pointin straight out like zombies. Their hands are on each other's shoulders, but there is still plenty of distance between them. My sister keeps them like this and has them move slowly in circles on her lap, doing some sort of a weirdo zombie dance.

"When are you going to start sending the money again?" my mom asks.

"Soon." My father looks at my mother. He nods his head like he's an honest politician. "I'll send it on my next check."

"How much will we get?"

"I'm not sure." My dad rubs his unshaven face. "I need some for rent and--"

"You need some for booze and you need some for the ponies." She stops. "Just send it!"

"I will. Believe me. I will."

"You always say that. But you never keep up." My mother honks the horn at some kid gliding through traffic on a bike. "First, it comes full for a few weeks. Then it comes for a few more weeks, only not so much. Then it stops." My mother stops the car at 47th Street. "You have to send more money. Please." My mother looks at my
father. Her face is pleading. She turns her face back to me. I quickly stare at the bottom of the car. "These kids NEED that money."

"I know. I will." My father lights another cigarette. As the car moves along, my mother watches traffic and my father stares out the window again. They say nothing else for awhile.

I decide to look out the window, too, hoping to see what my father sees. I don't see too much worth lookin at. Just cars and stores and billboards and sidewalks and people. I look at my father's face. I can see the side of it from where I'm at. He has too many wrinkles for his age and the skin covering his eye sockets is baggy and dark. When they liked each other, I thought my mom and dad looked good together. Her with the red lips, jet black hair and pretty face. Him with the wavy locks, blue eyes and tall frame. My mom still looks pretty. But the years have crept up far too quickly on my dad. He has teeth missing now, too, and his cheeks sag. He's only 40 but he looks like he could be someone's grampa. Every time I see him he looks older.

My mom parks the car in front of my dad's place. The race track stands tall across the street. "Welcome to Sportsman's Park," the sign says. No one's at the track yet. It's closed but still I can't stop myself from imaginin the sounds that jump outta the stands as the winners cross the stripe. I've never been inside my dad's place even though this is the fourth time I came with to drop him off. The outside of his place don't look so good. It has that kind of siding that looks more like it belongs on top of a roof. The wooden window sills are rotted and one window is busted out and covered over completely with wood and nails. The trash can on the corner, by my dad's front door, is knocked over. Thank God, there aint much junk in there. Just a little.

"Where's your car?" My mom searches the street with her eyes spread wide. "I don't see the Corvair anywhere."

"It's in the shop," Dad says quickly. "Er, ah, it needs some engine work." My mother bunches her face into a frown.

GI Joe is now flat to his back on the back seat. My sister makes Barbie jump up and down on Joe's chest, digging the heels of her plastic pink shoes into Joe's ribs each time.

"You didn't sell it, did you?"

"Hell no. I love that car. I'll never sell it." My dad pushes his bony fingers through his hair. "Like I said, it's in the shop." I couldn't tell if my father was lying. I don't think my mother could either.

"Did they take your driver's license again?"

"No-o-o-o," he says, dragging the word out til tomorrow. My mom turns her head away and looks out her side window. Dad looks at Mom. He wants to say somethin to her but he doesn't. His eyes are sad but he erases that glance quickly. He looks back at me and my sister. "Take care kids," he says as he grabs hold of the door handle. "I gotta get into my mansion before supper is served."

"Bye Dad," I say. Donna says nothing. She keeps her eyes on her dolls. My dad climbs slowly from the car and closes the door. My mom pulls quickly from the curb. I turn back and watch him. He walks right past the fallen garbage can and shoulders his way through his front door.

I snatch Joe away from my sister. Her eyes squint but she says nothing. Joe is, after all, mine. I grab Barbie and still Donna remains quiet. I lay Barbie on her back on the blue leather seat, her pointy boobs lookin at me. I put Joe right on top of Barbie and have him give her a great, big smooch. Donna likes this. Her grin is wide. So is mine. I start to move Joe up and down at the waist slowly. My sister's face freezes. Then I move Joe quickly, his hips banging against Barbie's hips.

"Mommmy, Mommmmy," Donna screams, "stop him!" My mom looks at me from the rear view mirror. I see tears rolling from her eyes. The warped smile on my face disappears and I drop the dolls to the car floor.

Holy Cross Hospital--Day 7

Mr. Alcott's been wheezing in a bad way all day today. He keeps that mask on his face, but it don't seem like its helpin any. Each breath he takes is a major league chore--like he's tryin to swallow a plastic bag or somethin. Everything sounds all tangled up inside that throat of his. I sure hope some of these doctors can help 'im. There's been bunches of 'em in here, buzzing around like flies on stink. A priest came to see Mr. Alcott today too. I closed my eyes when I saw that collar, pretending that I was asleep. But I cracked my eyes open a sliver to watch. The priest made it easy on me too. His back was to me so I didn't have no worries about him catchin me spyin. He's kinduva young guy--only about 27 or 28--with a thick head and no neck. He had those thick purple ribbons hangin offa that thick neck of his and he rubbed some oils from a tiny jar across Mr. Alcott's forehead and chest. He mumbled some words, words I knew were Latin, but I don't know what they meant. I don't know about God and all that, but if there is a God and a heaven, Mr. Alcott sure seems like the sort they should let right in. He don't have a bad bone in his whole body.

When the priest leaves, Mr. Alcott looks over at me and smiles. Then he pulls off his mask and opens his mouth. But no words come out. He's sure tryin to say somethin, but those lips are just cracklin and smackin like he's a mummy who's just been woke up after a 1000 year nap. I edge up on my bed and twist my body to the side. I lean on my elbow and stare. Mr. Alcott takes a big gulp of air and says, Have. He stops talkin and shoves the mask back on his face. He sucks in some big breaths and then pulls the mask off again. Have a good, Mr. Alcott says this time, but then he stops again. He coughs out a few bad coughs, real bad coughs, the kinda coughs that let me know today might be his last day. He slides the mask on and settles himself, taking four big, long breaths. His belly is covered up by those sheets but I can still see it floatin up and down with each breath. Mr. Alcott yanks that mask off again and spits out one last word, Life. He smiles my way again and slides that mask back in place.

Thank you, Mr. Alcott, I say. I will, I say. I for sure will try to anyway. He nods his head and then lies still in his bed. I keep an eye on him. His eyes close but he isn't dead. That stomach and chest are still both shakin. I lie back in my bed and try not to sleep. I am afraid of what I might see in my dreams. I keep lookin over at Mr. Alcott and keep tryin to stay awake. I do not want to see Mr. Alcott in my dreams. I know what my dreams will show me. But sleep comes any way. And yes, Mr. Alcott is there. He's dressed in a dark, pin-striped suit standing in what looks like a park, with green grass and trees all over. The sun has settled upon his shoulders and he is enjoying the warmth. He has a lit cigarette in his right hand. But then I notice that this is not a park. Amongst the grass and trees, tombstones and markers jut out. Mr. Alcott is staring down into a flat gravestone but for some strange reason, it's covered with snow. It has to be at least 75 degrees out, but still there's snow on this lone marker. Mr. Alcott drops to his knees and starts to wipe away the snow. The stone is made of gray granite. I see a name on the stone, *Foley*. Mr. Alcott pushes more snow off of the stone. It says, *Loving*. I yell at Mr. Alcott to stop. I scream as loud as I can. I know who that stone belongs to. It's my father's stone and I do not want to see it again. Not now. Mr. Alcott turns and looks my way. His face is clean-shaven, his whisker stubble a mere memory. I have to do this, he says. Again he stares into the stone. He slowly pushes away more snow and I see a year etched in the granite, *1960*. Oh my God, my heart begins to beat rapidly. I am still sleeping, but somehow I am utterly aware of everything. Sweat begins to form on my forehead and tiny beads slip down my face. This is not my father's stone. This is my gravestone. And then my body begins to shrink. I begin to grow smaller. Or could it be something else. Yes, it is something else. I am not growing smaller. The cinder block walls are movin in on me, slowly shaping, forming, pressing the walls in all around me, like a makeshift casket. Mr. Alcott continues to wipe away the snow, but now he uses only a single finger. He traces a *D* in the marker, followed by an *E*. Next comes an *N* followed by its twin. Stop, Mr. Alcott, I scream. Please, please stop. Mr. Alcott does not stop. My heart continues to pound, sending trombone notes bouncing throughout my body. The walls continue to push in. Mr. Alcott's finger falls upon the snow again, ready to trace the last few letters. That's when I snap awake in my bed, sitting up straight. Feet are pounding all about my room. So many heels are clickin, it sounds like my room's been invaded by a platoon of marching soldiers. When I shake completely to, I see white coats everywhere, circled all around Mr. Alcott's bed. Once they notice I am awake, the nurses push my bed away and pull a big curtain around Mr. Alcott. Hang in there Mr. Alcott, I yell. I use my sheet to wipe the sweat from my forehead. I do not yell again. Instead, I try to send Mr. Alcott a brainwave message, but I don't get any transmittal back. All I get is a long, flat beep. They roll Mr. Alcott away, people crowded all around him, and he doesn't come back that night.

Peaches

Gramma Foley's brain didn't work so good, so she lived in the old folk's home. She had some kinda disease that made it so she forgot most things, and since her mind didn't work so good, I never quite knew if I should believe a single word she said. Mom took us kids to visit Gramma three or four times a year. Johnny and Tim were ready to leave the old folks home the minute they set their teenage feet upon the beige linoleum floor. They'd park their butts on a couch, point their penny loafers at the front door, and hope the half-hour moved quickly. That's how long we always stayed. One half-hour. Never more than that.

Mom would always tell us kids to wait in the cafeteria while she went to get Gramma from her room. Sometimes it took Mom awhile to get Gramma ready. She might hafta help Gramma into her pajamas and robe, or Gramma might decide she wanted my mom to comb her hair. I never minded the wait though. There was always lots of old people to look at. They were staggered about the tables and chairs in the cafeteria like lost toys waiting to be put away. Some smiled at us, some just cried, some stared off at the lime green walls, and one guy--we called him Cow--liked to make mooing sounds all the time. When we got tired of starin at the old people, we kids busied ourselves calling each other "jerk" or "spaz" and then chasing each other around the room. That usually got Cow to stop mooing. He'd open his mouth wide and cackle away at our antics.

If Mom was real slow getting Gramma back, we'd ask Cow to show us his false teeth. He was only too happy to oblige. Johnny and Tim even joined us at the table for this. Taking one's teeth out should've been a quick thing, but it wasn't for Cow. He'd shuffle to and fro before us like a magician ready to tout his finest tricks, a big smile on his face. Cow was short, thin and wrinkly and he had two wisps of hair that stood tall on his head. He'd start by bowing and then he'd pull a white hanky from his pants pocket. Cow always unfolded the hanky slowly until a perfect white square draped in front of him, and then he'd swing that hanky, in a figure eight shape, through the air. Once he made a buncha eights, Cow would let go of the hanky and we'd all watch it float down like a feather, drifting from side to side as it fell, until it landed on the table where we sat. Then came the pointing. Cow would aim a skinny, wrinkled finger at the hanky, and keep that finger arrow-straight as he circled the entire table. He never said a word as he walked around our table. He just pointed. But that wasn't much of a surprise cuz I never heard Cow speak during any of my visits to see Gramma. Not a word. The only sounds that came from his mouth were mooing and laughter. When the pointing was done, Cow'd stand about ten feet away from the table, arch his body back as far as his old bones would allow and hold himself there a moment. Then he'd stretch his neck, thrust himself forward and cough his teeth out. And when those teeth came out, it was a thing of beauty. It seemed they were moving in slow motion, tumbling and twisting through the air like the acrobats you see at the circus. Cow's teeth always landed on that white hanky, most times right smack dab in the middle. That's when we kids would clap wildly for Cow and he'd take a final bow-- nice and slow like. Then he'd grab his teeth, dry 'em up with that hanky, and hand 'em to one of us. They were his top teeth and they were perfect little pearls stitched to bright red gums. There wasn't anything ugly or scary about 'em. Each one of us kids would hold the teeth in our hands, take a quick stare at 'em like they were precious jewels that shouldn't be held for too long, and then pass 'em along. When we all handled the teeth, Cow would shove 'em back in place, walk away and get back to his mooing.

We always knew when Gramma was getting near cuz we could hear her moaning at Mom. And then Mom and Gramma would appear from the hallway and Mom's right arm would be hooked around Gramma's left arm. Gramma always moved slow. She didn't so much walk as she shuffled, and her big fuzzy slippers didn't help her foot speed much. Her bath robe was always wrapped around her and the strap was bow tied at the waist. I figured Mom did that. Gramma wore a different colored bathrobe every year. Sometimes it was pink, sometimes white, and sometimes baby-blue. And she always had matching slippers. That's what we kids gave Gramma every year at Christmas, a new robe and slippers.

Gramma would start up the minute she set her eyes on us kids.

"I want outta this place," she'd say waving a finger at us. "I want out now."

"Easy, Mom. Easy," my mom'd say right back, "it's not so bad here."

"What do you know?" Gramma would look at Mom with pinched eyebrows and her thick black-rimmed glasses would climb up on her forehead. Her white, thinning hair seemed to bristle. "Ah-h-h, you don't know shit from shine-ola." You could always count on Gramma for a few good zingers and those zingers, along with Cow's teeth tricks, made the trip worthwhile for me.

"Have you ever eaten the food here?" Gramma would say. Her questions were the same every visit. I could rattle 'em off in the order they would come, if I set my mind to it.

"No, Mom. I haven't."

"Of course not. No one should. This slop isn't fit for pigs or even Eye-talians." Gramma liked to throw darts at the Italian folks. She probably would've died if she knew Johnny was dating one. Then she'd let things settle in for a minute. That's when all of us kids would line up in front of Gramma like she was Santa Claus, ready to hand out some presents.

"What do you want?" she's say staring blankly at us.

"Hugs and kisses, silly," Donna would say. And then Gramma would give us those hugs and kisses and then all of us, with our backs turned to Gramma, would wipe the kisses from our cheeks and then sit down. And once we sat down, there would be a brief moment of quiet before Gramma started in again.

"And I suppose it doesn't stink in here either?" Gramma'd say. She had us there. Truth was, the place did stink. It smelled like pee and disinfectant everywhere. It was so bad your eyes felt like they were on fire. Mom always lied to Gramma and I liked that cuz when I got in trouble for lying, I always told Mom that I learned it from her. She never punished me too bad then.

"I don't know, Mom. It smells a little in here, but it doesn't smell, too, too bad."

"Ah-h-h what do you know? You couldn't smell a fart inside a pillowcase."

Another one to add to Gramma's list. And that's how our visits to Gramma usually went. I say "usually" cuz sometimes, every third visit or so, Gramma would talk about breaking out of the old folks' home. She'd pull one of us little kids aside and say, "I'm breaking outta this place. You wanna help me?"

"Sure Gramma."

"Bring me a hammer and a screwdriver next time. Got it?"

"Sure do, Gramma." By our count, Gramma planned to break out well over 20 times. But she never did. She's still in that home now.

Whenever she asked me to bring the hammer and screwdriver, I'd have a little fun with her. I'd say, "Should I bring a saw too, Gramma?"

"Did I ask for a saw?"

"No, gram."

"What good would a saw do me? I'm breakin outta here. Not cuttin legs off."

"Right, gram," I'd say and chuckle.

And she'd look at me and smile and say, "You're a fine boy, Johnny." Only thing was--as you know--my name isn't Johnny. Gramma called all of us boys Johnny and she called all of the girls Jackie. "You'll make someone a great husband one day, Johnny. You have the face…of a mortician. Maybe that's the line of work you should get into."

"Sure thing, Gram," I'd say.

"Lotsa money in that mortician stuff, ya know. A never ending stream of clients. Remember. Shoot for the moon or it'll shoot you first."

"Right, Gram."

Mom said Gramma's brain went on shut down when her husband, Frank, died. That was way back in 1959, right around the time I was born. And things just froze up for her then. She remembered my oldest bother's name was Johnny, so she called all boys "Johnny." Gramma also remembered my oldest sister Jackie, so around Gramma, all three of my sisters answered to "Jackie."

Gramma always left us with loads of things to talk about on the ride home, like "What's a mortician, Ma? or "How do ya fart in a pillowcase, Ma" or "When's the last time you had some shine-ola, Ma?" By the time Mom got us home, she was ready for a breather. I don't know what wore her out more--Gramma or our stupid questions.

During one visit, though, a strange thing happened. Only Tim and I came with Mom that day to see Gramma. Tim played checkers with one of Gramma's friend's, a man friend. Gramma said he was her boyfriend. Sometimes she called him her "love-jockey."

"That's mighty nice of Johnny to play with old Ed there," Gramma said to me and Mom as she pointed to her man friend. "It keeps him away from me and I like that. Heaven only knows there's nothing worse than havin a soft, flabby dick chasin ya around all the time." Mom knocked her Styrofoam cup over and sprang to her feet. I nearly pissed into my shoes.

"I'll be right back," Mom stammered. "I'm gonna get a new cup of coffee. Do ya want anything, Mom?"

"No thanks, Jo. And take your time." Mom nodded. With Mom gone, Gramma leaned over the table. "I knew that'd get rid of her." She grabbed my hands and held them in her own. I looked at her hands. They were thin and wrinkled and full of bright blue veins. Brown spots that looked like huge freckles climbed all over her arms. She squished my hands and I stared into her eyes. For the first time in my life, Gramma looked as normal as any person I ever met. Just old. That's all.

"How come your father never comes with ya to visit, Johnny?"

I lied. "He's been busy at work, Gram." I lied some more. "Saturdays are his big work day." Truth was, my dad was sitting on a stool in a tavern somewhere. I knew it but she didn't.

"Is he sick again?"

"No Gramma." I decided to tell the truth. "He just came out of the sanitarium."

"What was he there for?"

"His ulcers. Liver. Lungs."

She shook her head and smiled. "He was always a sickly boy. Not like your Uncle Jim. He was always healthy. And most certainly not like Gene. That one was like a wild horse, even when he came outta me, kickin and scratchin and clawin. They had to open me up to get him out, ya know?" She laughed. "Not your dad, though. He slid out like a stick of butter." She laughed some more. "Got polio when he was 14." I didn't say anything. "You know that, right Johnny?"

"I knew he got it, Gramma, but I didn't know how old he was."

"14. I just told ya 14. Right?"

"Right, Gram."

"My God, Johnny. Get the Q-tips out and clean those wax mountains outta your ears." I laughed. Gramma did too. But then the smile left her face and her words came slow. "They told me, the doctors told me, that he'd never walk again. I listened to 'em but you know what I told them?" I aimed my eyes right at hers. "Bullshaven! That's what I said. He'll walk again, I told them. And he did. Everyone stayed up around the clock to help. We all covered a time slot. Frank, Ducky and Jim. Even Gene pitched in, back then, and he wasn't more than a half-pint like you."

"I'm no half-pint, Gramma. I'm 11."

She inched her face towards mine and turned her eyes into slits. "You're what I say ya are, Half-pint. Got it?" I nodded my head and then Gramma's scary look went away. She smiled again. "Anyway, we worked in shifts, ya know. We boiled towels in the water on the stove, rung the towels out and put these hot towels on your father's legs as he slept. And we massaged his legs with the hot towels when he was awake. It worked! They said it wouldn't work, but it did." There was a certain pride in Gramma's voice now. "We made it work." She stared deep into my eyes. "I wasn't gonna just sit there and let that son of mine be a cripple. No sir-ee, Bob! Two years after they said he'd never walk again, he was running down the street with all the other kids. Some nun thought up the remedy, ya know." She smiled. "Did you know your Aunt Ducky wants to be a nun?"

Aunt Ducky, her daughter, already was a nun. She'd been a nun for over 10 years now.

"Yes, Gram."

"You have nuns teaching you?"

"Sure do."

"Thank God for nuns."

"Yes, Gram." And that's how I came to find out how my dad learned to walk again, how he beat polio. He never said a word to me about those times. Neither did my mom, other than to say that Dad had the disease as a kid.

Mom came out from the hallway and walked toward us. She had a new cup of coffee in her hand.

"When's the last time you had a peach?" Gramma asked.

"'Bout two days ago," I said.

Gramma watched as my mom moved closer. "How'd it taste?"

"Good, gram. Real good. Cold and meaty, sorta."

"I haven't had a peach in so long." My mom stopped about 15 feet from us and fished through her purse. Then she pulled out the car keys. The half hour was up.

"I can bring ya one next time, if ya want, Gramma."

"That would be great Johnny. Just great."

A few moments later, Mom, Tim and me kissed Gramma good bye and as we started our walk towards the front door, Gramma wailed as usual.

"Traitors. All of ya. Leaving me here in this dump. You'll all go to hell in a hand-basket." We pushed our way through the front doors and walked for the car. On the ride home we laughed a bit over Gramma's antics, but it was laughter mixed with sadness too. We would rather have her out of that home, but we couldn't. Not with that disease that made her forget. Mom said Gramma was far better off in there cuz she couldn't hurt herself with someone watchin over her all the time.

We still visit Gramma at the home, but it seems we don't go as often anymore. Maybe just twice a year now. Gramma's not as feisty either. She's mellowed quite a bit. She likes to stare away at the lime green walls now and she doesn't say much. But whenever I visit, I always make certain I bring her a nice meaty peach. And I always give it to her just as we leave. She gets so wrapped up in that peach, she doesn't even see us leavin, and by the time she's done eatin it, she doesn't even know we were ever there.

Coupons

Dad musta won some money at the track. Sometimes he gets "hot tips," as he calls 'em, from some of the betters who come to his window at work. He stops by the apartment whenever he hits it big. Today, he musta hit a whopper cuz he just walked through the door to the Roach Motel with a five-foot-tall stuffed Panda bear under one arm and two small TV sets under the other. Donna snatches the Panda bear from Dad but not before saying, "Thanks Daddy." Dad never even said it was for her, but somehow she just seemed to know. The bear has baby-blue arms and legs, a white belly and chest, and a face and head that's a mix of both these colors. A tiny piece of red tongue sticks out from his mouth. Dad sets one TV on a kitchen chair. He puts the other TV on the kitchen table and plugs it in.

"It's color," Dad says. Sharon's in the front room with me. She looks at me with wide eyes and smiles. I fire a smile right back at her. We both jump off the couch and move into the kitchen, where we stand close to the TV and watch Dad play with the antennas to get the picture better. Donna could care less about the TV. She has pushed the bear up onto the lone chair in the front room and is talking to him. Little sisters! Who needs 'em? Within seconds, Dad stops fiddling with all the buttons. Every different color known to man spreads itself across the screen and makes the perfect picture. My favorite color is green. I stare into the tube and, for a moment, all I let myself see is green--the green, green grass of Wrigley Field. I feel sorry for John and Tim. They're out somewhere so they're missin out on this. Jackie's in her room listening to records with the door closed, as usual, and Mom's at work.

"How's that look?" Dad says.

"Great, Dad," Sharon says. She's still smiling. That smile hasn't left her lips since we jumped offa the couch. This is our first color TV and Sharon likes it as much as I do. The Cub game is over but the announcer, Jack Brickhouse, is talking to second baseman Glenn Beckert as part of the Tenth Inning Show. Behind them is that green, green grass I told you about. I've never been to Ireland but Gramma Roche says the greenest grass in all the world is there. Gramma's never been to Wrigley, though. Beyond the grass, you can see the ivy crawling across the brick wall, and the green seats in the stands. I love Wrigley Field. My uncle John took me there once. Believe me when I say that a black and white TV just doesn't do the trick. To really see Wrigley, you definitely need a color TV, and now I have one. After a bit, my eyes see the other colors again. The blue stripes on Mr. Beckert's uniform are as true blue as blue can be, and the big "C" on his uniform shirt is cherry red. Mr. Brickhouse is wearing a crazy looking sports coat that looks more like it belongs on top of a quilt maker's bed. It has little squares painted in oranges and reds and browns and grays all over it.

"What's the other one for?" Sharon says pointing at the other TV.

"You guys can use that wherever you want," Dad says. "Put it wherever. It's just a black and white, though."

I look at these two TV's and am thinking this is all pretty cool. We went from having an old busted down black and white TV that didn't work most times--cuz the screen rolled more than the wheels on my bike--to having two good TV's, one of which is color. Thank God for hot tips. Sure the screen is kinda small, probably a 12-incher, but still--it's color. Harry has a color TV too, cept his is a little bigger. Sharon and me sit in the kitchen chairs and just look at the tube. Dad stands beside us. Donna pulls her bear offa the chair and drags him across the wooden floor by his left foot.

"Don't do that, Kiddo," Dad says. "You'll dirty him all up." Donna keeps dragging the bear, making tiny circles in the front room. "Keep that bear off the ground or you'll—"

Donna stops dragging the bear and Dad stops talking. He keeps watching her though. Donna leaves the bear flat on the floor and climbs atop him, burying her head in his neck and throwing her arms around him. Dad shakes his head. "He's gonna become a brown bear if ya keep that up."

Donna twists her head Dad's way and smiles. She's missing a few teeth. "What Daddy?"

Dad shakes his head again. "Ahh, never mind," he says. He turns back to the TV.

Mom pushes through the front door. It's 6:00 now. That's the time Mom always gets home from her waitress job.

"Hi, Hun," Dad says.

"Hi, yourself," Mom says right back. She slips outta the wind-breaker she's wearing and sets it on the chair where Donna's new bear used to be. Mom is wearing a plain white shirt with short sleeves and a black skirt. She looks at the color TV we're watching and then at Donna and her stuffed bear. She pinches her eyebrows almost together and her eyes become slivers. "Big day at the track?"

"Sorta," Dad says. He looks at Mom and a slanted grin wedges its way across his face.

"'Sorta!' What do you mean, 'sorta'?" Mom says. Her voice is not so nice.

"Yah. Yah. I mean I won some money. That's what I mean."

I grab the other TV out of the chair and hold it up like a Christmas turkey. "Dad bought this one too." I am proud of my dad. It was nice of him to do these things for us and I want Mom to see everything that he bought.

"I hope ya paid cash for this stuff," Mom says. Dad doesn't answer. "Jack," Mom screeches. "Did you pay cash?"

Dad's voice grows soft and his words come slow. "Yah. I did. I paid cash. Mostly." He sounds like a kid in school who knows he's about to get beat up by the class bully.

Mom moves in towards us. She reaches her hand in at the TV and turns it off.

"Mostly?" Mom yells. "Mostly?" She wags her head. A fire-engine races away down 79th street, its siren screaming as it moves. Mom's voice seems almost as loud. I think maybe it would be nice if those fireman stopped here for a minute to put out this fire. "How much did it cost and how much did you pay?" Mom's voice is still loud. I know the neighbors can hear her. Mr. and Mrs. Escobedo are on one side of us. They can hear us, I'm sure, but they can't understand us. They're from Mexico, so they only speak and understand Mexican. The old ladies on the other side can sure hear us. Mom says they're nosy and never miss a thing. Well, she's sure makin it easy for 'em to not miss anything today. I don't know what it is about old ladies and apartments. They always seem to live in apartments. There's three old ladies in this one. Their mailbox says "Leonard" on it. There not nice old ladies like the O'Neil sisters from the old apartment that caught fire. These old ladies never say 'Hi', they never buy any of the raffle tickets or candy bars I hafta sell for school and Little League, and the tall one is scary lookin. She has a chewed-up face that looks like an old, worn out, sink sponge.

"Answer my question," Mom yells.

"Easy, now" Dad says to Mom like he's a cowboy talkin to a horse or something. "Everyone around here can hear ya?"

"I don't give a rat's ass who hears me." Mom points her finger around the room at the color TV and then the other TV and then the panda bear. She takes a deep breath. Her words come a little softer. "How did you pay for this crap?"

"Okay. Okay," Dad says. "I put some cash down and took out a coupon book for the balance." He pulls some skinny green papers from his shirt pocket. The papers are stapled together like the raffle tickets it seems I'm always sellin for my brothers. "I'm gonna send in a payment every month. And after eights month, the payments will--"

"Go on," Mom screams. Her face is now the color of the "C" on Mr. Beckert's shirt. "Get outta here." She grabs Dad by the arm, snatches the green coupon book from him, and pulls him towards the door. She stops at the front door and opens it. Dad looks at her like she's the only person in the world. Then he drops his eyes to the floor. "Now," Mom screams, only her voice is the loudest it's been. The word 'Now' flies out our door and bangs offa the hallway walls. The hallway says 'Now' several more times as the word clanks the walls of the stairwell until I hear one last 'Now' float out the entry door like a scared bird. Dad walks out the door and Mom slams the door shut.

Donna is still laying atop her panda. She has a look on her face like she hasn't heard a darn thing. She's sucking her thumb now.

"Coupon book," Mom says. She starts pacing around the front room. She snatches a pack of Winston 100's from her purse and lights one. She blows the smoke out fast. "Another bill." She moves some more and her black waitress shoes make it so her steps are soft and quiet. "That's just what I need. Another bill." She walks some more and takes another puff of her cigarette. "I love bills." She keeps walking in the front room, pacing back and forth. Mom's not talking to me or Sharon or Donna, so I figure she's talking to herself. She does that sometimes. I get the urge to see the green of Wrigley Field again. I snap on the TV.

"Turn it off," Mom screeches. "Right Now." She's staring at me like I just stole all her tip money. I look at Mom with an open mouth, unable to budge. She glides over on her silent black shoes and turns the TV off. "And don't touch it again, either. Neither of you. Hear me?" Sharon and me nod our heads. "We need to give these TV's back to Goldblatt's." She whirls around and looks at Donna. "And You," Mom says. She scoots over to Donna and pulls her off the Panda. "Stay off of this thing. Understand?"

Donna starts to cry. "But I like it, Mommy." She cries some more. "Why can't I just have it? Daddy's the one who gave it to me." Donna's tears keep coming. Mom walks past Jackie's room, where she is still listening to records with the door closed, and goes into Donna and Sharon's room. She closes the door and stays in there a good long while. She goes into Donna and Sharon's room when she wants to be alone. She can't go into her own room, cuz she doesn't have one. She sleeps on the front room couch. We all stay quiet in the kitchen. We are listening for sounds from Mom. I don't hear anything but the music from Jackie's room. I think maybe Mom is crying but I don't know for sure. Maybe she's just talking to herself again, trying to figure things out.

Eight months have passed and I'm still watching the Cubby games on the color TV. It's a new season now. I hope they do better this year. Johnny and Tim snatched the new black and white and set it up in our back bedroom, so we can watch the shows in there if we want, without any girls to bother us. Donna still lays all over that Panda, only he aint so white anymore. Like Dad said, that bear looks more like a brown bear now. Mom went and saw the Goldblatt's man but he wouldn't take the TVs or the Panda back. Mom worked a lot of extra days to make the money to mail in with those green coupons, and now the coupons are all paid off. Dad hasn't been back since he brought us our presents.

Dark Side of the Moon

I only saw my dad a handful of times after my mom kicked him out of the apartment that last time. And most times I saw him, I didn't really see him. That sounds kinda strange, I know. But it's true. Mom took us younger ones to every home basketball game at Leo High School, to see John and Tim play. They went to the same school that Dickie O'Brien went to and, like Dickie, they were both good at basketball.

Sometimes, Dad would be at the games. I'm sure it must've been a struggle for him to make it up all the stairs to get to the gym. Some bright guy put the gym up on the third floor. Anyways, we always sat where we were supposed to sit--with the home crowd, so we could cheer wildly. Whenever Dad turned up, he came nowhere near us. He pushed himself way up into the farthest of corners in the upper deck. He was so skinny and so far off in the corner that he looked like a large sliver sticking out from the wooden bleachers. Cept you didn't see many slivers with brown fedoras tilted across their wooden heads.

Whenever I saw Dad, I'd point him out to Mom.

"So," she'd say.

"So, don't you wanna talk to him?" I'd ask.

"Not really," she'd say. "If he has some wisdom for us, he can come over here and share it." Things were beyond repair between them. I was old enough to know that. But what kept them together? I often tried to figure that out as I stirred in my bed at night. I knew about divorce. Some of my friends at school had parents who were divorced. What kept my parents from doing it? Especially since Dad stopped sending any money at all to us now. Whatever money he made, he used on booze and the ponies. So Mom signed all of us kids up for Social Security. We got monthly checks. Problem was our government sent the first six months of checks to the wrong address. They sent them to Dad. He cashed all those checks with our names on 'em and kept the money for himself.

"That's how bad he is now," Mom said when she figured out what happened. "Not only does he not send money, but he steals from us too."

When the games end, Dad is always gone lickety-split. I think about going over to talk to him before the games end but I don't go. Mom'll get mad if I do. Sometimes, when I'm havin such thoughts, it's like Mom can read my mind.

"Go ahead," she'd say. "Go on over and see him." I'd start to move a bit, getting ready to go. "But don't come complainin to me when you get there and he's stone-cold drunk." Then, I'd sit back down and play it safe. So like I said, I saw my dad here and there, but then again, I really didn't.

After one game, Mom sent me up to the locker room while she took Donna and Sharon to the car. I was to see if my brothers wanted a ride home. I'd never been sent to the locker room before. Why now? I thought as I worked my way up there. My brothers never came home with us after a game. They went out chasin cheerleaders. Maybe I was givin it too much thought. When I made it to the locker room, I found my father standing there, just outside the door.

"Hey sport," he said. His brown hat was tilted back atop his head.

"Hi, Dad." He smelled of booze but he wasn't drunk. "What ya doin?"

"Ah, just waitin for a bit. Wanted to talk to John and Tim for a minute." Years later, John and Tim told me that dad sometimes waited outside the locker room for them after their games. They said he usually had some comments and suggestions about the game, some of which were actually helpful.

"How 'bout you?" he said, "what you doin?"

"Oh, Mom sent me up to see if John and Tim wanted a ride home."

"She did, did she?" He fingered the unlit cigarette in his left hand.

"Yah."

"Tell her, No," he said matter of factly. He peeked into the locker room. He had a smile on his lips when he turned back. "I'm sure these guys are going out with their pals or something."

"Okay, Dad." I turned to leave.

"Hey sport, you ever seen a black moon?" I turned back.

"A what?"

"A black moon."

"No." I had no idea what he was talkin about. Maybe the booze was startin to take effect.

He nodded towards the locker room. "Peek in there and you'll see one."

I looked into the locker room and starin me square in the face was Austin Gill's butt. He was less than ten feet away. He was the darkest of all the black guys on the basketball team. He was changing out of his uniform and stood tall, his butt completely bordered in white by the straps of his jock. And those white straps made his butt seem even blacker. I made a twisted face. I had been buying Johnny and Timmy new jocks and socks for Christmas for years now, but I never actually saw a jock on either of them, and I most definitely never saw one wrapped around some black guy's butt. I was frozen.

My dad pinned himself against the wall with laughter.

"Go tell your mom that you've seen the dark side of the moon," he said between chuckles. "She'll love to hear that." I just shook my head back and forth as I walked away, muttering, "Idiot," to myself.

Public School

Father Mac said he liked me, but he had to do what he had to do. After another fight, he kicked me out of St. Colletta's. Mom signed me up for McCord Public School. I had to do the fighting thing there, as usual, and that got me off on the wrong foot with Mr. LoCallo, the principal. But what's a kid to do when he's the new kid and guys test him out? You put up your dukes and protect yourself. Right? That's what I did alright but I was tired of it. I was tired of new schools and new apartments and having to prove myself all the time.

The best thing about the public school was Harry. We were together in the 5th, 6th and 7th grades. But that wasn't such a good thing, at times, cuz we always got in trouble when we were together--which meant that we had loads of punishment sentences to take home. It seems I was forever writing, "I promise never to . . ." or "I understand that it was wrong to . . ." You get the picture. Anyway, my mom and sisters helped me with the punishment writing. We would all sit around the kitchen table at night, and write out the punishment sentences. I could hold three pens in my hand at once and thus write three punishment sentences at the same time. It's amazing how a brain works when it has to. Mom asked me to try harder to be good in school and I promised I would. Try, that is.

Fifth grade was when they first sent me to the speech therapist. I actually started stutterin in the fourth grade. Any word starting with a "W" or an "S" was an utter chore for me to get out. St. Colleta's didn't have anyone to work with stupid, stutterin kids like me. McCord did and just in time too. In the fifth grade, my stutterin was real bad. I don't know why it started or how. It just did. So once a week, I walked into a tiny office that was painted the brightest pink I ever did see and the speech therapist worked with me on my W's and S's. That was right about the time Grampa started coming over to the Roach Motel twice a week to have me read to him, too. Grampa would prop me up in his lap and have me read a short story to him. It was magical. No matter how often I stammered on a word, Grampa didn't flinch. He never told me I was a retard or anything, like Johnny always said when I hit a fit of the stutters. Whenever I got caught on a troubling word, Grampa would just pat me on the leg, gently with his talking hands. Over and over he'd pat me, every story night, helping me work though those W's and S's. His talking, tapping hands always said, "It's okay. Take your time, Dennis. You'll get it. You're doin just fine." And I was gettin better too. I think Grampa's method easily helped the most. The speech therapist at school continued to work with me, but she did get mad when--one day--I asked if I could sit in her lap and read to her.

The sixth grade found me running straight-forward into Mr. LoCallo. Harry and I were fond of teasing this little Lithuanian kid named Eddy Lisauskas. We weren't bullies looking for kids to mess with. It's just that it was hard not to mess with Eddy. He liked to wear white button-down shirts and he always tucked them inside his underwear, even after he just took a fresh dump in the school washroom. We first noticed Eddy's stained tails in gym class. Then it was all over. After that, we were forever chasing Eddy around the school, pulling out his whitish-brown shirt tails for all to see. Mrs. Lisauskas had a talk with Mr. LoCallo and Mr. LoCallo had enough of us. He gave us one last chance to stop. We didn't. Then one afternoon, near the end of the school day, the announcement lady said, "Harry Everest and Dennis Foley, please come see Mr. Locallo immediately." We did. We laughed our way into his office, glad to be out of class.

Mr. LoCallo was there, seated behind his shiny black desk with his big hands in front of him. He smiled at us. His hair was white and his teeth big. "Follow me, boys," he ordered. We didn't know what was in store but we were certain it was going to be funny. We were wrong. Mr. Locallo led us to the supply room, where--of all things--the school supplies were kept. The sign on the door said so. Harry couldn't let that go.

"Hey, Mr. LoCallo," Harry said pointing at the sign on the door, "is that why they call this the supply room, cuz this is where the school supplies are kept?" I busted out laughin. Mr. LoCallo smiled and walked over to the door. It was open. He closed it and then walked over to us. He grabbed us by our hair and clanked our skulls together. Moe, Larry and Curly woulda been proud.

"Hey, what's that for, you—" I started. Wham! A full fist with a big, bumpy ring on it right to the gut. I fell to the ground and gasped for air, my fingers rummaging about the beige linoleum floor. I thought my insides were falling out. A moment later, Harry was at my side doing the same thing.

"That's a warning," Mr. LoCallo screamed. "You two little shits better stop fucking off, or you'll be meeting me in this supply room every damn day." He opened the door and left. The door slammed closed and we heard the turn of a key. Harry and I stayed on the ground until we caught our breath. I then stood up and checked the door. We were locked in. The three-o-clock bell rang 15 minutes later but no one came for us. We heard all the other kids leave for home. We dared not make a sound or we'd be in for more of it. The clock on the supply room wall kept us posted. Harry and I didn't talk much. We mostly watched the hands of the clock turn. At 5:30, the key was put back in the knob and the door opened. Mr. LoCallo stood in the doorway.

"Do we have an understanding, boys?"

"Yes, Sir," Harry chirped immediately.

"Yes, S-s-s-s-sir," I added.

"Good. Go on home now. The front entrance is open. Make use of it."

We ran home together, sprinting the whole way. Harry ran into the Igloo amidst a scream from his mom of "where the hell've you been?" I entered my apartment. Mom wasn't in from work yet, my brothers were at basketball practice, and the girls were watching TV. No one said anything when I came in. I wasn't missed. I grabbed my mitt and ball, went outside, and fired some pitches at the box on the wall.

Holy Cross Hospital--Day 8

When I wake up, there's still no Mr. Alcott in my room. Tracie comes to check on me. I wanna ask about Mr. Alcott but I don't. I'm afraid of the news. She gives me some eggs and juice and she fluffs my pillows too. She looks over at my tube. It's still clear. There hasn't been any blood passing through it for two days now. I think I'm all drained out. Tracie reads the look on my face and talks. Yes, she says as she sit's beside me, Taylor Alcott died last night. Still no family has come to the hospital. I don't eat my eggs or drink my juice. I just sit quiet all day, even when Mom comes, and stare at those 2-foot by 4-foot ceiling tiles.

Why you still here? I say to Tracie when I see her later in the day, just before I go to sleep for the night. I'm workin a double, Tracie says. I'm on til midnight. Tracie sits with me and we talk. I ask her about college and she tells me it was the greatest experience of her life. Tracie played volleyball in high school, so we talk about that a bit too. And then we talk about basketball. We cover a bunch of other topics too, for about a half hour. But we don't talk about Mr. Alcott. I like Tracie. A lot. I'd like to marry a girl like her some day. She's easy to talk to, she's pretty, and she's smart. Not a bad combination, huh?

Get some rest, Sweet Pea, Tracie tells me when she gets up to leave. A good night's rest, she says, and you might be ready to say goodbye to the ICU tomorrow. I watch Tracie walk away. I can never get enough of that wiggle. She stops at the light switch by the door, and aims her eyes my way. He was a nice man, wasn't he? I stare at Tracie, unable to answer her simple question. I know the answer, just like you know the answer. The answer is, Yes, Taylor Alcott was indeed a good man. He was a very good man. But I can't get my lips to move. They are sewn shut. I swallow some air and nod my head at

Tracie. Then I bury myself in my sheets and covers. Tracie turns the lights off and heads out the door. There's just two emergency lights on now. They always stay on. They're a pair of glowing eyes that see and know all things, and now they're starin into my soul ready to steal my secrets and unleash my fears. I pull the sheets up over my head to block those eyes. I hope they don't bring anyone new into the ICU. It's better that way. I don't want to meet someone and start to like 'im, like Mr. Alcott, and then have 'im die off on me again.

Mr. Brunner's House

Mr. Brunner is the name of the guy who lives next door to Harry. Sometimes he has beers with my dad at the tavern when my dad's around. He's not married and he's gone a lot. Harry's mom says Mr. Brunner's a traveling salesman. All I know is Harry and me like Mr. Brunner. He gives us $5.00 every week in the summer and fall to cut his grass and he let's us use his push mower too. Harry and me have a system. I cut Mr. Brunner's front yard and Harry cuts the back yard. We both rake up after ourselves. $2.50 a piece every week is alotta money. More than I've ever had. Me and Harry don't have to steal the penny candies from the store anymore.

Since Mr. Brunner isn't around much, sometimes me and Harry sneak into his house when we know he's gone. We climb in through the side window closest to Harry's house. The window slides up nice and easy-like, and there's lots of bushes right there so it's hard for anyone to see us. We don't go in to steal. No way. That would be wrong. We just go in to check things out, and believe me when I tell you that Mr. Brunner has lotsa things worth checkin out. Every wall in Mr. Brunner's house is painted chocolate. Harry says he likes it but I think it's weird. The rooms all feel small and that brown makes it like the walls are movin in on ya. Mr. Brunner has one of those fancy, new water beds in his bedroom. Neither me or Harry has ever seen such a bed before. We lay on the bed whenever we sneak in and try to cut farts, cuz farts sound a lot different on a waterbed than they do on a mattress. Try it sometime if ya don't believe me. You'll see what I mean. Other times, while we're on the water bed, we just close our eyes and shake our bodies and make believe we're Huck Finn and Jim floating down the Mississippi on a raft. Now I'm all for playin on a water bed, but I doubt I could ever sleep on one, not with all those miniature waves rockin ya back and forth all the time. I'd like to ask Mr. Brunner what it's like sleepin on that bed, but Harry says I can't do that cuz Mr. Brunner might get suspicious. He's right, too. On the basement walls, Mr. Brunner has some framed pictures of him in an army uniform with lots of other army guys around him. Their faces are all painted up in greens and blacks and they have rifles in their hands. There's a glass bookshelf in the basement, too, and on it there are four medals. Above the medals is a framed picture with words only in it. It says Gone But Not Forgotten. Bring our Viet Nam POW's Home.

We spend most of our time in the front room. Mr. Brunner has loads of nudie magazines on his coffee table. That's what me and Harry like to look at. Whenever we're in Mr. Brunner's house, we snag a mag, plop ourselves on the chairs in the front room and just stare away at the naked ladies. I used to not care much about that furry area between the legs, but I wanna know what that's all about now. Harry says that ladies grow fur between their legs when they get to be about twenty-years-old and the fur stays there until they have babies. Once those ladies have kids, Harry says, the fur falls right off. Sounds like a winner to me. You should see the front room lamp Mr. Brunner has. It's a table lamp that's shiny gold in color and shaped like a naked lady with big boobs, cept there's no head where the head should be. That's where the light bulb goes. Before we leave, me and Harry always rub the boob lamp for good luck. Hey, you never know where a Genie might be hidin, right?

We don't sneak into Mr. Brunner's too often cuz we don't want to get found out, and we don't say a word to the other kids on the block or from school cuz we know they'll ruin it for us. Me and Harry sometimes play with Schraeder and Booger, two other kids on the block, but we don't play with them too much. Booger lives in the middle of the block and Schraeder lives right across from Harry. Booger's family is from Tennessee and they all talk funny. They all got that twang thing happening. Booger calls me Dinnis, even though I keep tellin him my name is Dennis. Johnny says Booger and his family are Hillbillies. He says all of Burbank is filled up with Hillbillies like them. Booger's got a black dog in his back yard called "Blackie," but I stay away from that dog. He's nuts. Anytime I'm around him, he starts humpin all over my leg like he aint seen a lady dog in a zillion years. He leaves everyone else alone. Lucky me, I guess. Booger says it's my red hair that sets Blackie off. Booger's real name is Butchy Snegg but we started callin him Booger after we found out he stole a twelve-pack of Pepsi offa Harry's back porch last Summer. That's the main reason why we don't play with him much anymore. We're sure Schraeder had somethin to do with it, too. Like me and Harry, those two are always together. Schraeder's big and scary-lookin like a zombie. He has a long, flat face like a jumbo pancake, and he almost never smiles or talks.

Whenever me and Harry play Mumbly Peg, we always call on Booger and Schraeder. We like to watch 'em chew on mud. To play Mumbly Peg, you dig a little pit out of the grass about six to eight inches deep and about a foot wide, and you fill that pit up halfway with water so it gets good and muddy. Then you start by slammin your pocket knife into the pit. If the blade sticks into the ground, you pick someone else to dig out the knife, using only their mouth and teeth. As the game goes along, you hafta make the knife do little twists and flips in the air before the blade sticks in the pit. If you mess up and the blade doesn't stick in the ground, you don't get to pick someone to dig. You hafta get the knife yourself, and when that knife is layin flat in the water, you're gonna come up with a mouthful of mud. I guarantee it. That's why we like gettin Booger and Schoeder to play. Anyone can make the straight-ins stick in the pit, but it takes some skill to make the blade stick, after you make it flip and twist. Me and Harry have that skill. Schraeder and Booger don't. So guess who goes home with the dirty teeth all the time? That's right, the Pepsi thieves.

Our Mumbly Peg pit is right below Mr. Brunner's side window, the same window that me and Harry sneak through. After Booger and Schraeder got their teeth dirtied up good during Mumbly Peg one particular day, I don't know what made me say it--but I did, and once I said it, I couldn't take it back.

"Hey, you guys wanna sneak into Mr. Brunner's with us?"

"Hey," Harry snapped. His chin almost fell into the Mumbly Peg pit.

"It'll be okay," I told Harry.

"What do ya'll mean, sneak in?" Booger said.

"We'll climb right in the window here," I said pointin my finger. Harry wagged his head. "He's got some good magazines in there, if ya know what I mean. And a water bed." I flashed my teeth. "Tell 'em about the magazines, Harry."

"No," Harry said. "You tell 'em. You're the one with the motor mouth."

"Y'all bin in there before?" Booger said. I nodded my head. "Does he have inny C-gars in there?"

"Not that I've seen," I said. "But great magazines, believe me."

"I'm fer it," Booger said. Schraeder nodded his head and remained speechless like the zombie he was.

Well, that was the day I learned that some secrets are better off not being shared. We all climbed into Mr. Brunner's house and I gave Booger and Schraeder a tour like it was my very own castle. I showed them the waterbed, and the medals and the basement posters. Then we took our seats on the front room couch and chairs, and had a good, long stare at the magazines. When we were done with our readin, we all rubbed the lucky boobs before we left. On the way out the window, Booger landed in the Mumbly Peg pit. He screeched and rolled around on the ground like someone had just chopped his leg off with an ax. Once he quieted down, he limped home with a sprained ankle. Booger musta told his mom how he hurt his leg cuz soon thereafter, when Mr. Brunner came home from out of town, Booger's mom had a nice chat with him. And the next thing we knew Mr. Brunner had an alarm system put in his house, and he told me and Harry that we couldn't cut his grass any more. I was glad Mr. Brunner didn't say anything to my mom or Harry's mom. He could've got us in some big trouble, if he wanted to. His refusal to squeal on us made me feel even guiltier about sneakin into his house. I also knew that I'd never get to ask Mr. Brunner about the war and all his medals neither, cuz I couldn't muster up the courage to even look at, let alone speak to, Mr. Brunner anymore.

Harry and me sure miss havin that money in our pocket. It hurts even more now that Mr. Brunner's new grass cutters are Schraeder and Booger. I don't know how they worked that one out. After all this, Harry made me promise that I'd never let out another secret, ever again. I swore to it and crossed my heart. That's the best anyone can do as far as promises go.

Foot Rub

The last time I saw my father alive I had just turned 12. But Dad didn't come bearing any belated birthday presents. He took me to the tavern. Imagine that. Like I told ya before, I was long past enjoyin taverns. Popp's Tavern was long gone. It left with the last white folks in the old neighborhood. We went to a tiny tavern in Burbank at 79th and Mulligan named, Shot-n-Beer Joint.

Dad only had two drinks that day. Screwdrivers. Heavy on the OJ. Apparently he thought if he couldn't smell or taste the booze, it meant it would go easier on his derelict liver. Two drinks. That's all he could take. I don't remember anything he said that day. I wish I did. I don't even know if we spoke. I just fed dimes into the pin ball machine to kill the time and kept askin, "Can we go yet?" When we left the tavern, Dad was flying. Even after just two drinks. His system could no longer handle any more. On the three-block ride back to the apartment, the few times I had driven a Go-Kart came in mighty handy. I had to grab the wheel on the Corvair twice to keep my dad from crossing over into the eastbound lanes. When we finally parked the car and climbed out, Dad wrapped his arms around my waist and shoulder and I helped him up the stairs. He was broom stick thin. I was skinny but he barely had me by a few pounds. Once inside, Dad plopped himself on the couch and took off his socks and shoes. I turned on the TV and sat in a chair. When I looked over at Dad, he was already out, looking long and lean and barely alive. For some unknown reason, I stared at his naked feet. His toes twitched as he slept and he moaned words I couldn't quite make out. As I watched him, I was filled with a desire to hate the man. The way he was--was bad for my mom. She deserved better. Still, I couldn't find the hate within me. When his toes twitched again, my mind slipped back to our last Christmas together. We were at Uncle Gene's house. He's my dad's youngest brother. Though drink was plentiful at the party, Dad didn't have a drop the whole night. He was out of the sanitarium for over a month at that point and hadn't had a single drink. I think he really wanted to stop. He was so proud of himself. On the ride home that night, my mom drove and my dad sat next to her. Mom still had the '65 Galaxie then. I sat in the back seat with Donna and Sharon.

"I did pretty good tonight, didn't I?" he said, his eyes smiling, his soft voice seeking approval.

Mom smiled right back at him. "You did real good, Jack." There was hope in her voice. She turned her eyes back to traffic. "Real good." Her hand slid slowly across the blue leather seat and grabbed hold of my father's sickly fingers. Dad stared at her hand and the car moved along in silence. Then Dad's shoulders shook and the tears came. He sobbed like a little baby. A few moments later, the tears were gone. The hands stayed joined and my mom rubbed her thumb back and forth tenderly across Dad's palm. I nodded to my sisters. All three of us stared at the joined hands from the back seat, not quite knowing what to think. Mom didn't drive my dad to his place that night. He stayed at our apartment and he didn't sleep on the couch either. Mom made Jackie sleep on the couch.

But that was almost six months ago. Dad was back to drinking again, and he'd already bounced in and out of the sanitarium twice in that same period. His toes twitched again. There was no way I could hate this man. In my heart, I knew he wished he could change things. He just didn't have the willpower to do it. He was my father, sink or swim. I walked over to the couch, lifted Dad's feet up, and slid myself beneath them. I pulled his feet across my lap and massaged his toes one at a time, starting first with his left foot. He sighed long and hard like an old hound and then slept without any further sound. When I finished with the left, I worked on the right. And when the toes were done, I massaged the balls of his feet and worked my way up to his ankles, the ankles that were part of his polio stick legs. I worked on him as best I could until I fell asleep on the couch with Dad's feet still atop my lap. When I came to, Dad's pencil legs were gone and so was he.

Holding Hands

My mother's hands were in my hair.

"Dennis, wake up," she said softly. I shook to and looked to my right. Johnny and Timmy's beds were empty. Saturday night had turned into Sunday morning. They were still out. The overhead light was on. I shaded my eyes with hand cover as I looked into my mother's face. Mom moved her lips but no words came out. She tried again but still no words came.

"What, Mom?" I squinted as I spoke, still hiding from the overhead light.

Mom smiled. It was a rather shy smile, the same kind of smile Mary Phelps gave me two weeks ago when I asked her to go to the seventh-grade soc-hop with me. When my mother's smile vanished, I wondered if it was ever there. It was gone that fast. She chewed on her lower lip, and horizontal lines cut their way across her forehead.

"Daddy died tonight," she finally said. She ran her fingers slowly through my red locks again. I stared into my sheets. I didn't wanna see her face. I didn't wanna know if she was relieved. "Say your prayers for him." She paused. I could feel her eyes upon me. I refused to look up even though I knew she wanted me to. "He wanted to be a good man. I know he did."

She rubbed my back for a moment and then stood up. I continued to stare into my sheets. Mom flipped off the light on her way out of my room. Then and only then did I look up. She walked down the hallway and stopped outside the room where my sisters, unaware of the news they would soon receive, were still fast asleep. The hallway light threw my mom's shadow against the wall. It was long and bent. My door was open part way. I couldn't see my mother but I could see enough of her shadow to see it shake and tremble. Tears fell from its eyes. Then I saw light from Jackie's room hit the hallway. In seconds, Jackie was on her feet and went with Mom to Donna and Sharon's room. I heard Mom whisper some words and though I couldn't make out the exact words, I knew what was being said. Donna started to cry.

"It's okay. There, there, now, Donna. Heady downs, heady downs," Mom said, borrowing the Irish phrase that was passed down from her own mother. I didn't have to be in that room to know what my mother was doing. She was patting Donna's head softly over and over again. Sharon and Jackie were silent. They were playing the strong game, too. As Donna continued to wail, I jammed my face into the pillow. I would not allow myself to cry for if my mother had to be strong, I, too, would be strong. Sure, her shadow could cry but she did not. I prayed uncountable Our Father's and Hail Mary's and others into the night. Then I stopped.

"I hate you, God. I hate you." No, I didn't hate God for taking my father. I knew it wasn't God's fault. The almighty one didn't open my father's mouth and pour endless streams of booze down it. My father did that of his own choosing. But still, I wanted to say good-bye. Why couldn't I at least be able to say good-bye? I wanted to be at the hospital. I wanted to hold my father's hand and tell him that I loved him. I wanted to tell him I loved him, for I knew just as I had never heard those words from him, he had never heard those words from me.

"Good night, Daddy. I love you. Good night, Daddy. Good night. God, I'm sorry. I don't hate you. Sorry for saying that. Good night, God. Good night, Daddy. I love you both." SLEEP.

And that night as I sleep, my father is in my dreams. We walk about talking, laughing, hugging and playing games of sport and chance. Never do we go to the tavern. Never does he have a drink in his hand. Never do I have to walk home with him and help him up the stairway. I tell him he loves me and he says the same. When I wake up, I am sad but I am happy too. I look forward to seeing my father in my dreams again. And I do. At least 3-4 nights a week, I receive dreamy visits from Dad. We go to Cubs games, he helps me work on my curve ball, he helps me with my math, and he tells me about girls and their parts--which is of great interest to me. Always we are holding hands. Always we say we love each other before we part. I am sad my father is gone but I am having more fun with him now that he is dead. I look forward to each night's sleep.

"Daddy loves me, Mom," I tell my mother one night, a few weeks after Dad's funeral, as she tucks me in. "He really loves me." Mom smiles at me and pats my head. I smile back and then close my eyes. I am ready to sleep for I know that soon I will be holding hands with my father.

The Black Limousine

I jabbed two fingers between the slats of the aluminum blinds and pulled down lightly. Through the triangular crack I made, I looked out the window at the street. The black limousine wasn't there yet. All I could see was the front of Schraeder's house and a stretch of empty street. I pulled my fingers out and the blinds snapped back to attention with a bang. Tim coughed and then cleared his throat, all the while tugging away at his collared shirt and black tie. Johnny picked a piece of white fuzz from his sport coat, using his right index finger and thumb like a tweezers, and then flicked the fuzz into the air. I watched the fuzz float slowly away like a tiny star no one would ever discover, until it disappeared into the wooden floor. My sisters all wore dark dresses that fell below their knees. All of my brothers and sisters were sitting in the front room of the Roach Motel, their faces blank, their eyes staring emptily at the hardwood floor. Mom was on the kitchen phone giving someone directions to the funeral parlor.

I let my eyes wander the room until they stopped at a picture of my father resting in a frame upon the top shelf of the front room book case. That photo had always been there but I never really noticed it before. It was an old black and white photo, my dad's Confirmation picture, and he was decked out in a dark suit and an even darker tie. I walked to the book case and stared. A tiny roach crawled across the frame and stopped atop my father's ear to sniff with its tentacles, before disappearing again. The photo made my father's blond hair white, but still it blended in easily with the golden frame. The smirk on Dad's young face told me he wasn't too excited, back then, about having his picture taken. And I knew how he felt. Exactly. After all, at the time, I was about the same age as the boy in that photo. Again I cracked the blinds open and looked. Still no limo.

* * * *

I was but six when I went to my first wake and funeral. It was for my Aunt Debbie. Actually, Aunt Debbie was my Mom's aunt and my great aunt, but to us she was still just plain ol' Aunt Debbie. My brothers and sisters all came to the wake. Mom dressed us in funeral duds, little black suits for the boys and frill-less dresses for the girls. Mom held my hand when it was our turn to visit the casket. Dad held my sister Donna's hand.

It was all so strange to me then. I remember finding it odd that men were smoking and talking and laughing in the hallway lounge outside the parlor. Someone was dead. I thought it was time to be sad. The tears wouldn't come from me, though, mind you. Truth be told, I didn't even remember ever seeing Aunt Debbie while she was alive. I just remember hearing her name in family stories. She was my grandmother's sister and, like Gramma, Aunt Debbie moved to Chicago from Ireland. But Aunt Debbie became a Northsider. I'm sure my gramma kept up with her but not me. The Northside was far away to me back then. It was a whole different world. But still, I remember thinking that men should not have been laughing and smoking with Aunt Debbie just fifty feet away, laying in her casket bed. I knew enough to wear a sad face.

Dad and Donna visited the casket first. She was only three then. Their kneeling time was cut short. Donna started reaching into the casket with her bony little arms to touch Aunt Debbie, and kept sayin, "Wake up, old lady, wake up." She spoke so loud, everyone noticed. The blue-haired, old ladies in the second row of seats wagged their heads. Dad snatched Donna into his arms and quickly made his way out to the lobby. My brothers, John and Tim, went next. I watched their every move. They pressed their knees into the kneeler that stood before the casket and crossed themselves the right way, from forehead to belly, and then left shoulder to right. I still couldn't get that right at the time. They were smarter than me, but that was to be expected. They were six and seven years older. After crossing themselves, my brothers pushed their hands together in the prayer position, put their hands on the velvet kneeler rail, and bowed their heads before the casket. They knelt there for awhile. When they were done, they crossed themselves again and stood up, sad looks painted on their faces. Jackie and Sharon went next. I didn't watch. They were girls and, as a boy, I figured there wasn't much you could learn from watchin girls at the time. And then it was my turn. I knelt down in front of the casket, Mom at my side. I crossed myself slowly, trying to remember which shoulder to tap first. I got it right and was glad. Once I looked at Aunt Debbie, it was all over. I couldn't stop myself from staring. I thought I'd be afraid. After all, John and Tim used my first trip to a casket to tell me about all the wakes they had been to and how the dead guys sometimes reach out from the casket and grab ya by the throat.

As I looked at Aunt Debbie, I knew she wasn't going to grab me. She was in a far away sleep. Her hair flowed long past her shoulders and was as white as only snow can sometimes be. She wore a tiny grin on her powdered face. That's what I'll always remember most about Aunt Debbie. That grin. Her lips were smooth and straight but they turned up at the edges forming this handlebar grin I speak of. Since she was smiling, I knew then that death wasn't such a bad thing.

When mom stood up from the kneeler, I did the same. She grabbed my hand and we slowly walked away. We stayed at the funeral parlor for several hours after that and I must tell you that I snuck a buncha visits back to the casket. I just had to see that smile again. Aunt Debbie was dead but she was smiling.

She knew something I didn't know and I thought if I stared at her long enough, I'd figure it out. I didn't.

At the funeral the next day, I was the only one who came with my mom. I don't know why the others didn't come. All I know is that my mom was the Lone Ranger and I was Tonto. Everyone else stayed home with Dad. Mom borrowed a neighbor's car for the funeral. We had a car back then, but it was all dented up. The car we borrowed was a shiny, '64 Mercury Monterey, the one with the rear window that tilted the wrong way and went up and down. All during the ride out to the cemetery, I played with the button that controlled the rear window, making it go up and down and up and down, but Mom didn't seem to mind. Mostly I kept the window down, though, to get some wrap-around-breeze in the car. It was a scorcher. There were cars in front of us and behind us all during the trip. All of the cars kept their front lights on and stayed close together like freight train cars joined at the hip. There were no neon orange funeral stickers on the cars back then. No one thought up that lovely idea just yet. When we entered the curvy streets of the cemetery, that's when I first caught sight of the big black limousine. It swung into my view.

"Wow, Ma, look at that car, "I said aiming a finger. My mom smiled and nodded. "It looks like the Green Hornetmobile." My mom said nothing. The road swerved the other way and my eyes followed the limo.

"Who owns that car, Ma?" My mom still said nothing. I asked again.

"It's rented," Mom finally said, and that was it. It was then that I noticed that her mind was elsewhere. Sure, I didn't care much for Aunt Debbie, but my mom sure did. Years later, I learned that Aunt Debbie lived with my mother's family for several years while my mom was young. Gramma helped her get on her feet when she first came over from Ireland and Aunt Debbie became my mom's childhood confidant.

"How do ya rent a car, Ma?" I stared at her sad mug. Mom stared ahead but answered.

"The family rents the car." She pulled the steering wheel slightly to the left as we bent with another curve. "Her husband died long ago, before you were born. He was a nice man. His name was Jim. So now, it's her kids, my cousins, who are in that car." She took a deep breath and released it. "They're the ones who rented it."

"Why Ma?" Her answer came quick.

"Maybe so they don't have to think about driving. So they can just think about their mom. Someone else gets hired and drives for ya."

"Kinda like rich people, huh, Ma?"

Mom laughed. "Yah, just like the rich people."

The hearse came to a stop in the curvy road as did the big car behind it. We climbed out of our borrowed car and walked toward the hearse. Just then, the doors to the limo swung open. Legs wrapped in pin-striped trousers and others in dark stockings stepped from the car. The legs from the limo stayed close together, even as they moved near the hole dug in the ground, and the hands above the legs were linked together for strength like strands in a rope. The faces above the arms were sad and wet and I knew then that these people knew Aunt Debbie much more than I did. Aunt Debbie wasn't just some lady in a casket. She was somebody who others loved, loved enough to miss and cry over.

A priest walked to the front of Aunt Debbie's casket, his green and white vestments blowing in the wind. When the priest said his words, I felt Mom's right hand tighten around mine. I looked up at her and saw tears fall freely from her eyes. I squished her hand back. I then decided to try to cry, too. If my mom was crying over Aunt Debbie, then Aunt Debbie was certainly deserving of my tears. I tried and tried, thinking of every sad thing I could think of, but no tears came. Not even after I thought about smushed puppies layin dead in the street.

* * * *

The blast of a horn rattled the front room window. I jabbed my same two fingers back into the blinds and opened the familiar hole. The black limo sat along the curb in front of the apartment. The limo windows were dark and I saw no head inside. Sunlight slipped through the clouds and landed on the front grille. The chrome shined like well-polished teeth. Aunt Debbie again raced through my brain. And then I thought about the other wakes and funerals I had been to after that. There always seemed to be some distant relative or old uncle from Ireland that had died off. Though I was only 12 at the time, I was already a professional wake-and-funeral-goer. Old ladies with starched, white hair, black dresses, too much lipstick, and thick obituary scrapbooks had nothin on me. It seemed I was forever marching through the solid wooden doors that stood in front of all of God's funeral parlors. I drove through endless miles of curvy cemetery roads, my eyes always fixed on the limo.

The horn sounded again. Mom was off the phone. She had a scowl on her face. "Beep the horn and rush me, will ya?" she said loud enough for all of us to hear. She grabbed her purse and strode towards the front door. "That bastard'll get no tip from me." With my brothers and sisters, I stood up, walked stiffly behind my mother and prepared for my very first ride in a black limousine.

That limo ride came and went and I don't remember a single thing about it. Not a thing. I don't even know if Mom stiffed the limo driver. He deserved it, if she did. He should know better than to rush someone who just had someone die on 'em. I can't tell you much about my dad's wake or funeral either. Truth is, my brain went on shutdown. There are only speckles of information that flash before me. Fleeting speckles.

I can tell you that my mother never left the greeting line at Dad's wake. She was setting the example. For two whole days she stood there, baggaged in black, and greeted everyone who came to pay their respects, her face blank as a store mannequin. Only twice during the two-day wake did I see tears roll down my mother's face. Then and only then did she look more alive than my father.

I remember flowers. At Dad's wake, the smell of fresh cut flowers invaded my nose. The attackers came from every conceivable angle. All about the room, flowers bloomed. And I swear I saw some of the flowers move. Really. There were carnations and roses and lilacs and tulips and more. Everywhere there wasn't a chair, a couch or a person, there were flowers. Some flowers stayed low to the ground in decorative pots while others climbed high on white trellises. Some flowers climbed so high, their petals covered the many gilt-framed paintings of Irish towns that roamed the walls. Flowers. Yes, I remember the flowers.

All the aunts and uncles and cousins came to the wake and funeral, and they all brought their sad faces and dark suits and dresses with them. But I can't get myself to see the faces of all the others who knelt before my dad's casket. I still can't see my dad's face in that casket, either. My eyes wouldn't move past his hands. But I do remember those hands. They were caked with powder and wrapped with thick black rosary beads that looked more like chains. Dad's fingers were so skinny I thought they might break off whenever someone reached in to touch them. I didn't cry at the wake or funeral cuz Johnny told me, "men don't cry." So I didn't. I was a man after all. Like I said, I was already 12.

I do remember when Gramma Foley came to see her son. They brought her in from the old folks home where she still lived cuz she couldn't remember anything or anyone anymore. But oh, she remembered her son, her oldest, her pride and joy. Uncle Jim ushered Gramma Foley to the casket, and she showed everyone that her brain wasn't as far gone as everyone thought. She looked at my dad, her son, and ran her fingers over his face, his chest, his powdery hands. I watched it all from the side, in that line that I hated to stand in cuz everyone who walked past you told you they were "sorry for your loss." Gramma Foley shrieked and crumbled.

"My boy…my baby…my Jack. My dear…dear Jack. My good…good boy." She would not, could not, forget her son, the oldest--the one she willed to beat polio and walk again. "Is he really gone?"

Uncle Gene claimed his mother's other arm. And as Uncle Gene and Jim walked Gramma Foley away, Uncle Jim said, "Yes Ma, he's gone. The good die young, Ma. The good die young."

I tell none of my friends that my dad died. Since he wasn't around too much, no one really notices that he's missing. Two other kids at school had a parent die on 'em during the school year and it was broadcast over the loud speaker announcements. The school even held fundraisers for the families. We tell no one at our school. We don't need their sad eyes and we don't need their sad money, either. I don't even tell Harry. I just spend my time firing strikes at the box on the wall on my way to becoming the neighborhood fast-pitch king, the mitt Dad gave me always stapled to my left hand.

Holy Cross Hospital--Day 9

Yee-hah!! They moved me from the ICU to a regular room today. Tracie gave me a nice kiss on the forehead before I left. She handed me a sealed envelope too. I figured it had a card inside it. Open it later, Tracie said. In my new room, a doctor came to remove the tube. Mom was there for it. I wasn't sure what to expect but I sure expected some pain. The doctor took off the tape surrounding my tube and then snipped the stitches. A nurse stood at his side. She pulled some tape off of a roll. It was a great big piece of tape, thick and wide and white. The doctor told me to take a deep breath and hold it. I did. He yanked the tube out of my side and the nurse covered the hole with the tape. She then added some more tape. It didn't hurt at all. I swear it. Two more days, the doctor said, and you can go home. Mom said, Thanks doctor, I'm anxious to get him home. The doctor patted my head like I was some cuddly dog before he left.

I like not being sewed up to a tube. Now I can walk to the bathroom for a squirt or to bake the loaf. No more bedpans. Yippee. I am told to stretch my legs and walk the halls. I do. It feels so strange to be on my feet again. I never realized how good it feels, just to have feet and legs and to be able to use them. After my walk, I'm dog-tired. I climb back in bed to rest. Mom says goodbye and leaves. I tear open that envelope that Tracie gave me. There's no card inside. It's a sheet from the Tic-Tac-Toe game which Mr. Alcott folded into fours. The games I won on that sheet are circled. On the bottom of the sheet, it says, You're a winner. Don't ever stop trying. It's signed, Taylor Alcott. I miss old Taylor Alcott. I sure hope he made it to his fantasy land.

Later in the day I am told I have visitors. I figure it's the boys. I'm wrong. A Mr. Taylor Alcott, Junior and his daughter would like to see me. Isn't this interesting, I think. Perfect timing. I say come on in. And as I wait I plan my words. I'm gonna yell at this man and say, What the fuck? The old geezer waited and waited and you were a no-show. Taylor Alcott, Junior and daughter will feel guilty when they leave me today. Believe me, they will. I would give anything, even my newly repaired lung, to say goodbye to the dead. I put on my best mean face and wait for Taylor Alcott, Junior and daughter.

My mean face goes away fast when I hear why Junior didn't show. He was goin through a divorce. Tracie talked to his soon-to-be-ex-wife when Tracie called on the phone that time, only Tracie didn't know anything about Junior's personal life. The soon-to-be-ex-wife never gave the message to Junior--until after Senior was dead. She wanted to screw him one last time. Junior didn't get the other messages either cuz he was living elsewhere. Senior didn't know about Junior's divorce cuz Junior didn't have the heart to tell his dad. When Junior stopped over to his dad's place and found it empty, he called all the local hospitals and that's how he found out that his father was dead. Then his wife told him that she forgot to give him the message. Sorry, she said to Junior. Yah, right, Bitch, I'd like to say to that lady. What kinda move is that?

Taylor Junior and his daughter are nice people. Taylor Senior should be proud. I tell them how I felt like Senior and I were talking though brainwaves at first. They stare stupidly at me. When I tell them that I read some newspaper stories to Senior and he liked it, their faces brighten. Junior says I'm a nice kid. I tell them that Senior's last spoken words to me were: Have a good life, and they cry. I join them. And then I show them the Tic-Tac-Toe card with Mr. Alcott's words on it and we all cry some more.

Green White and Orange

Not long after my dad died, it was time to break out the funeral duds again. As I stood in the greeting line with my uncles and brothers at the second night of the wake, two men approached. None of us had ever seen them before. They said they were in from New York. They were old, they were Irish, and they wore overcoats that were as long as their grief-stricken faces.

One old man shook my Uncle Mike's hand and said, "We're here to do the honors." He held a flag folded into a triangle in his left hand. The other man nodded and remained quiet, until he saw me. He released a thin smile, stooped over and spoke.

"Was he your granfar?" he asked. His face was a face that had seen many things. I could tell that right away.

"Yes, sir," I said.

"Sorry for your loss, son." He reached over and sandwiched my right hand between his huge paws, paws no doubt that had worked many a year in the fields of green. The tears that gathered 'round his eyes told me his words were true. "I knew your granfar many, many years ago when we were both young like you. I was with him the day he left home, too." His brogue was wonderful. It soothed my soul.

I glanced over at Grampa Roche, resting in his casket, waiting patiently to shake hands with God. Why didn't you tell me you had friends, Grampa? I thought. Why didn't you tell me about your days as a boy with this man and your days thereafter? I would have loved to have heard those stories.

Gramma and my mom walked over to greet the two men. After introductions, Uncle Mike asked the two old men to join him in the break room, out of earshot of the women. I tagged along after my uncles and brothers.

It was all rather strange at first. We stood in the break room cloaked in utter silence, staring at the dark blue wallpaper that wrapped all four walls. Others, not in the immediate family, sat on chairs and smoked. But even they were strangely silent. Uncle Mike kept looking at the two men and then back at the flag that rested in the wrinkled hands of the taller of the old men. I had never seen a group of Irishmen so quiet for so long. After a bit, everyone turned their eyes to the wooden floor and stared at their shoes as they slid them back and forth. Finally, Uncle Mike spoke. His words came slowly and softly.

"My dad was a quiet man. He said very little. Truth is, I don't know much." He swung his head towards the rest of us. "None of us do. We only have our suspicions." He then aimed his eyes at the flag and said, "Tell us why you're here." The taller man, a Mr. Ryan, glanced at me. "It's Okay," Uncle Mike said, "he can hear it too." I felt very grown up but that was of little consolation. Grampa was gone. His heart of quiet gold finally ran dry. He was 72.

"Now, I don't know what you boys know about your da," Mr. Ryan said eyeballing Uncle Mike and Uncle John, "or your granfar," he said as he turned his eyes to Johnny, Timmy and me, "but the short of it is--he was a hero." He twisted his head to his sides and stared at the others seated in the break room. His words became a whisper so all of our ears leaned in towards his lips. "Michael joined the IRA when he was 15. He gave us many years of nothing but excellent service. Never was there a mission he didn't accept. I could go on and on, as could Mr. Killeen," he said turning his face to the shorter man, the man who had shaken my hand. Mr. Killeen nodded. "But I'll tell ya simply this. If your da, your granfar had it his way, I doubt he ever would have come to the States. He was told to go. I told him to go." Mr. Ryan stopped and sucked in a big breath.

"He was a hot ticket back then, he was," Mr. Killeen added. This time it was Mr. Ryan who nodded his head. "I grew up with Michael. We both lived in the town of Templeglantine. We worked together for years." He stood silent for a moment as he scratched at his chin. "It was a sad day when he left Ireland. Sad for me. Sad for him. Sad for his parents." And then there was silence again. Long silence.

I wanted more. This was good, but it wasn't good enough for me. This was our only chance to learn more about the man who said so little, the man who spoke only with his hands. This little bite of information did not satisfy my hunger. Someone tell them to talk more, please, I beg you, I thought. Uncle Mike musta heard my brainwaves. He spoke.

"Tell us what you can. Please. Whatever you can." The two men looked at each other as if deciding what to say and who should say it. Mr. Ryan took the honors.

"Your da, your granfar was caught several times for gun-running." His voice was still a whisper. "He was one of our primary runners in the South. He and Mr. Killeen handled the countryside outside of Limerick City. When he was caught the first time, he was imprisoned in Limerick Jail. It wasn't much of a stint, maybe six or eight months or so." He paused as all of our faces worked hard not to show surprise. "But the last time he was caught, he got twenty years." His eyebrows grew tall upon his face.

"That last time they sent him to Droichead Nua, not a pleasant place to be," Mr. Killeen said. His face sprang to life as he spoke. He didn't look so old any more. "Michael went on a hunger strike. I got the word through one of the guards. I knew Michael would rather die of the hunger than rot in that prison. I couldn't let that happen. That's when I contacted Mr. Ryan. He gave us the Okay. On the eleventh day of the hunger strike, we sent in a crew to break Michael out and break him out they did." He stopped to again scratch at his chin. "Problem was, if you view it as a problem, a guard was killed during the escape."

Uncle John asked the question on all of our minds. "Did my father kill the guard?"

"Now I can't say he did or he didn't," Mr. Killeen said. "Truth be told, I just don't know. No one there that night, including your da, your granfar, claimed the act. But the British authorities pointed the finger at Michael. He was the prisoner. He was the easy target." Mr. Killeen dropped his chin and stared into the floor. "He was only twenty-two at the time."

"We got him passage to New York two weeks later," Mr. Ryan said. "He was too hot to keep. Someone would have gotten to him. I made him go." Mr. Ryan raised the flag to his chest. "That's why we're here lads. The Republic of Ireland wishes to honor your da, your granfar, Michael Roche. He fought for what he believed in, a united and free Ireland."

With Grampa gone, the bottom fell out for me. I knew my world would never be the same. I was almost 13. My grandfather was a great man in my eyes. He was quiet and strong and always there when I needed him. And that was enough for me.

By this time, my stuttering was barely existent, thanks to Grampa. Two years and hundreds of stories had passed since he first sat me on his lap and had me read to him. I asked to read a poem for Grampa at the funeral mass. I got the Okay. In church at the pulpit, I unfolded the poem I wrote for him. I called it, "The Greatest Man I Know." As I read the poem, tears raced from my eyes, dampening the paper, but never once did I stutter. The New York men brought a flag to honor Grampa. All I had was a stutter-free poem. But that was the only way I could think to honor the man who was always there for me, always there for all of us.

Gramma made frequent trips to Ireland, but Grampa, the fugitive, was never able to return to the land he loved. That must have hurt him so. I wish I knew about his years in Ireland so I could've talked to him about it while he was alive. I don't know about heaven and all. Maybe when you die, you go to your favorite place. If that's so, I'm sure Grampa's resting somewhere upon the green, green grass that birthed him, a book resting in his lap, waiting to help all the little stutterin boys of Ireland.

When they closed Grampa's casket, Mr. Ryan and Mr. Killeen unfolded the green, white and orange flag, the flag of the Irish Republic, and draped it across the bronze box. It rested easily and looked very much at home. There was utter silence in the funeral home at that moment, with all eyes staring at the flag. Uncle Mike now has that flag tucked away in his closet. One day, I hope perhaps, it will be mine.

With Grampa gone, my dreams are no longer pleasant but they are constant. Always I see a clown face with red hair and a blue nose. I am at the circus by myself, no family around, enjoying it, waving to the elephants, acrobats and clowns. Then a clown turns sharply and stares at me. He does not have a clowny face. Sure he has bright, floppy, neon red hair, a pasty face and a blue nose, but his slits for eyes are evil, his look sinister. He runs up the steps towards me and points an accusing, Uncle Sam-like finger.

"You, I want you," the clown always says. I jump from my seat and run. I make good distance between us, since he is slow because of his floppy shoes. Then I hit a patch of cement and get stuck running in place. He gains on me.

"You, I got you," he says as he lunges for me. Always I break from the cement and run again. I race to the ladder leading to the high wire. The clown discards his costume and I can see that he is a witch decked out in the blackest of black. Sometimes the witch is a man and sometimes the witch is a woman. There is no broom and the he-she witch climbs up the ladder. As the witch nears me, he-she roars with laughter, "You are mine," and as the witch's hand reaches for my shoulder, I jump. Always I jump. And as I fall I know I am going to die. Closer, closer to the ground I fall, and then, just before I splatter, I awake and I am alive. I have that dream hundreds of times and always I awake before I splatter. I know who the monster is who is chasing me. It is death. My father and my grandfather are gone and if I do not behave myself, I know with the utmost certainty I will be next.

Over the next year, I am not quite myself. I am polite, I behave, I do nothing wrong. I am a saint. I was never an extremely bad boy, but now I am an exceptionally good boy. I stop with the curse words and I start my old tricks too. I stop looking at my pud when I pee or bathe cuz I might die for it, and I stay away from the girls and the nudie books. When my friends start talkin about Raquel Welch, I just walk away. If I look at dirty pictures of big boobed ladies or talk about the same, I know that within days I'll be laying in a casket.

Shortly after Grampa died, we move away from Harry to a new place. My mom gets re-married and we live in a house for the first time. From birth, I have now moved nine times, but I can only remember six. I like the new house, even though it's out in the burbs, and I like the new man. I am still very, very good for one more year. But then I go to high school and guess what? Michael "Spud" Flynn's at the same school and so is Harry. I introduce Harry to Spud and Spud gives us intros to Bobby Molloy, Pat Finnegan, and the O'Grady twins. All the guys start callin Harry--Hairdo, cuz of his thick black locks. Harry likes his new name and we all become fast friends. Things are spinning, churning, changing within me, screaming to get out. I decide then that I no longer want to be a very good boy.

Like Fathers--Like Sons

I hit it off with Bobby Molloy right away. He was on the freshmen basketball team at St. Laurence with me. I stayed over at his house one night and had my very first beer. Bobby was 15 then and I was still 14. Spud met up with us too and so did the O'Grady twins. We drank in an alley over near Marquette Park and we all had three or four beers and split some Boone's Farm wine. I never thought I'd like drinking, but I do. Truth is, I didn't think I'd ever touch the stuff. You know why. But it's not so bad. Really, it's not. I sure don't like the taste much at all, but it's worth gettin over that bad taste to get that feeling you get from drinkin--that silly, stupid, invincible feeling. No wonder my dad liked to do it so much.

I hang around with Bobby and Spud and the others on weekends. We always go out drinkin. Since I live far away, I usually stay over at Bobby's or Finn's or with the O'Grady's. I meet their parents. All of the fathers like their booze. A lot. They always have a beer or a drink in front of their face at home, or you see their cars parked out in front of the taverns that line 63rd Street.

All of the moms and dads tell us to behave when we go out, except for Mr. O'Grady. He sits down at his kitchen table every night and drinks. Whenever I stop over, I sit with him. Alotta times, Finn's there too. The O'Grady twins and Finn are cousins. Mr. O' is most generous with his beverages. He gives us beer to drink and he even mixes up the booze drinks for us. Anything we want is A-Ok with him. He's the only parent I know who lets us guys drink in front of him. He treats us like the men we are.

My mom tells me not to drink. "You don't wanna end up like your father, do ya?" Mom says. Sometimes she picks me up and drives me home after I been out all night. To hide the booze smell from her, I chew on breath mints and gum, and if I have neither, I just pull up some green, green grass and chew on it and hope and pray that some leg-lifting dog hasn't been using that same grass lately.

Every Friday and Saturday night, I meet the boys on the front steps of Hubbard Public High School, at 62nd Place and Hamlin. That's our usual meeting spot. I ride the bus in from the 'burbs to get there. That's where my step-father moved us. The rest of the guys are all from the neighborhood. The stairs at Hubbard are made of thick concrete slabs and the landing's large enough to hold twenty kids at once. Once we're all there, we pool together our dollars for the beer. Once the money's all set, it's always me and Bobby that head off to get the beer. Armanetti's liquor store, just off 63rd and Pulaski, is a three block walk. When we get to Armanetti's, it's my job to pick out a runner. Now, pickin a runner is a definite skill, an art in and of itself, and if you don't think so, you better get your brain examined. If I pick the wrong guy, he'll pocket the money for himself and leave us without the happy juice for the night. And what are we supposed to do then, drink grape juice? Or maybe call the cops and issue a complaint? Yah, right. Of my friends, I'm the only one who hasn't been burned by a runner.

Bobby and I wait in the Armanetti parking lot for the right guy. We eyeball everyone who pulls into the stall. I stay away from the fatherly types. They probably have kids our age at home who are busy doing their homework, so they'd never buy for us; and besides, they might just call the cops on us. I stay away from old-timers too. They always seem to be mutterin to themselves as they make their way towards the door. I can never quite figure out what's going through their minds. I look for young guys with sunglasses or leather jackets or bandanas. A guy wearin all three is a definite winner, and so is any guy wearin cowboy boots. Also, anyone trying to look like Elvis is a top rate buyer. He'll never turn ya down. Whenever you come up on a runner, you gotta make sure the guy at the Armanetti cash register can't see ya. That's why me and Bobby stay in the back of the parking lot. Once I find the right guy, Bobby hands him the money and we always give 'im an extra buck or two for his troubles. Once the runner buys our beer, we always walk the alleys back to Hubbard. You see, high school kids walkin down the street with cases of beer in their arms don't go over too good with most people, especially the cops. If the cops catch you with beer, they'll take it from you and give you a big lecture about the evils of alcohol--and then they'll have a few laughs at your expense later that night as they drink your beer. Believe me. I know. The cops have tagged us before and skipped off with our brew. That's why Bobby and me always stay in the back alleys on our way back to Hubbard.

Most nights, after we get our beer, we drink in the alleys or in the schoolyard. There's all kindsa cool ways to drink beer. Chugging, shot gun, and with a straw, to name a few. Harry's favorite is with a shot glass. He drinks a shot every minute. One little shot a minute doesn't sound like much but--you know what--a six pack is gone in just over one hour. I like watchin Harry do his shot-glass-a-minute thing. He parks his butt on the ground and pulls his little Irish cap over his eyes to concentrate. He lines all of his beers up like soldiers before him and sets his stop watch between his legs. Then he gets after it. Harry can knock off a twelve pack in two and a half hours if he feels like it. Bobby likes to collect the plastic six pack rings. He folds em up, making one thick ring, and then pulls the rings apart like the muscleman that he is. He can break twelve rings at once. I can only bust open eight at once.

Finn and Bobby have girlfriends. They go out with the McMurray sisters. Finn's a bad stutterer. He's far worse than I was when I was young. Finn likes it when I get drunk. I still can't say my "W's" or "S's" when I'm skunked. It's like I'm a little kid again. Finn just laughs then. He says it makes him feel good. After the drinkin, Bobby and Finn usually grab their gals and go smoochin. Not me. I go lookin for fights. Spud's always with me. Always. We are a definite team. We always know what the other's doin, just like when we were little kids. Now if I throw a little crap Bobby's way, he'll hold off on his smoochin and come with me and Spud. We'll fight anything that moves. Mostly, we beat up the longhairs from the public high school, from Hubbard. Sometime's I'll crack some kid who just happens to be struttin down the street. Don't get me wrong. I don't beat up on little kids. Only kids my age or older. And I never go after old people. I am respectful to them. That's how our Fridays and Saturday's usually go. Drinking and fighting. I like to do both cuz I'm good at 'em. I can drink a twelve pack now without throwing up and I've never lost a fight. It's important to be good at stuff. You know that. I'm good at basketball. I start for my team and I'm good at fighting and drinkin. That's a pretty good set up. Sure I like the hoops, but I like fighting better. You make a mistake in basketball, the referee whistles you and calls a violation or a foul. In fighting, there are no referees and there are no rules.

Harry's mom dumped their Burbank house and bought a house a half-block away from the O'Grady twins. Lucky guy. He's in the neighborhood with Bobby, Spud, Finn and the O'Grady's now. It's funny how things and people come together. I'm the only outsider now. But that's alright with me. I know I'm really an insider. I belong. I'm tough and I can drink.

Sausage and Eggs

Spud invited me to stay over at his house. I've stayed over at everyone's house, except Spud's. I have to stay somewhere. There's no buses heading my way after 10:00 p.m. Sometimes I feel like a mooch, so I don't ask anyone if I can sleep over. On those nights, I go to the apartment building at 63rd and Pulaski, give Big Chief, the huge cigar store Indian on the Northwest corner, a salute and then sleep in the hallways. As long as I settle down after 2:00am or so, no one is up and about to mess with me. I can have a nice little snooze for myself. Every now and again, I'll find a garage to snooze in. One time Mrs. Lally found me sleepin on the old beater couch she keeps in her garage. She's just another white-haired, old lady from the neighborhood who happens to leave her garage unlocked. I was sound asleep, laid out like a stiff on her couch, when she found me on a Sunday morning.

"Holy Mary, Mother of God," she yelped. That woke me up. I jumped outta that couch and sprinted past Mrs. Lally. Her face matched the color of her hair. I was long gone before she knew it. Mrs. Lally doesn't know me since I don't live around here. But she doesn't leave her garage unlocked anymore.

I've been tryin to avoid Spud's house. You know why. But I don't wanna hurt the little guy's feelings so I tell him, I'll stay over. And guess what? I came over to Spud's after school and we chased squirrels with Shep his dog before leaving to meet the guys at about 7:00. No Mr. Flynn anywhere. Thank goodness. Mrs. Flynn was nice, though. Very inquisitive, but nice.

"Sorry to hear about your father, Dennis."

"Thanks, Mrs. Flynn."

"How long's he been dead now?

"Three years." Spud and I were at the kitchen table gnawing on ham sandwiches, chips and dill pickles, the dinner of champions. We both sucked on milk shakes too. I'm a firm believer in milk shakes. So's Spud. They coat the belly before a night of booze.

"And how long ago did your mother remarry?"

"Two years ago, Mrs. Flynn."

"I see," she said. And then she went silent, playing with her chin like she had whiskers.

We met the boys at Hubbard. We drank our beer but no fights tonight. We all got smoochy with the girls instead. I played kissy face with Maggie Vonderlynn. She's a good smoocher. I like the way she wiggles that tongue in my mouth. I wiggle my tongue back at her. I don't want to let her have all the fun. But she smokes too and I don't like that ashtray-in-the-mouth taste much at all. Why would someone wanna do that to their mouth and lungs? During the walk home, Spud told me about his kissy face. He was with JoAnne Healy on the side of the school. JoAnne not only did the kissy thing, she let Spud play hide the finger. Or so he says.

"C'mon," I said. "You shittin me."

"Nope," Spud said, a proud smile on his face.

"She let you put your finger in there?"

"Yep."

"What'd you do with your finger?"

"I moved it back and forth inside her like year sposed to, ya dumb fuck." I said nothing. I tried to picture Spud with his finger in the spot. I couldn't. All I could see was Spud stickin his finger in a light socket and then gettin shot across the room, amidst sparks and fire and smoke. "She liked it a lot," Spud added. "She even grabbed my hand and helped me move it around."

This was too much for me. After that Suzy Egan stuff, I was very off limits with girls' bodily parts. Kissing was fine. The tongue thing was A-OK, too. But I didn't think it was good to play with girls' parts or for them to play with mine. That's dirty.

Lookin in nudie magazines at girls is fine, but you shouldn't look at, or touch, any such parts on a real girl. I wanted to have a good girlfriend, one I could respect and smooch. I don't want a smoker--like Maggie, or a finger girl--like JoAnne. But still, in a weird, dirty, inquisitive way, I liked Spud's story. I kept my ears open.

"When I was workin on her, she started rubbin my sausage from the outside."

My eyebrows shot up. "Are you bullshittin me?"

"No." I looked at his pants and eyed his dick area.

"I don't see no stains," I said pointin.

"Cuz I didn't make any stains, dip-shit. I never said I went."

"Watch who you're callin 'dip-shit,' ya dwarf." Spud chuckled. So did I. Then I shook my head back and forth. Yep, Spud was full of B.S. He was pullin my leg.

"I think you're fulla shit."

"Oh yah?" Spud said. I nodded my head. "Well take a wiff a this." Spud stuck his right index finger beneath my nose. I sniffed at it and immediately knew that he spoke the truth. I never smelled anything like that before, but his finger smelled just like I was told the spot should smell--fishy. I told Spud I believed him.

"Damn right you believe me." Again he cracked his proud smile. We turned down the alley where we played as kids, opened the back gate and came upon his garage. I stopped to peek in the window. Spud kept walkin, but stopped when he discovered I was no longer at his side. My eyes were busy searching.

"He aint in there no more," Spud said. I turned and faced him. He walked towards me.

"Who?"

"I know what you're looking at."

"What?"

"The fridge." I turned my head and nodded. Spud peeked through the window with me. An alley lamp gave just enough light to see the freezer section of the fridge.

"Did your dad find him . . . in that bag . . . in the freezer?"

"Nope."

"What happened?"

"I buried Finch, like you said." His words came easily. His eyes were still aimed at the fridge. "It was the right thing to do. You were right. I buried him up near the Marquette Park Lagoon."

"Good," I said. "Good." We crept quietly into the Flynn house and slept on mattresses on the basement floor.

In the morning, Mrs. Flynn woke us for breakfast. Mr. Flynn wasn't at the kitchen table. Score another one for me. Mrs. Flynn said she was cooking sausage and eggs. I said, "Great." Spud said, "No thanks." He was always conscious of his weight during wrestling season. He helped himself to a small bowl of cereal. We sipped a cup of tea at the kitchen table while Mrs. Flynn stood at the stove. I was ready for a hearty breakfast and felt sorry for Spud and his measly bowl of cereal.

"So how's your grandmother?" Mrs. Flynn asked.

"She's doing good. She likes livin with us." Gramma Roche moved into our house with us after my mom got remarried to John. I filled Mrs. Flynn in on all of my gramma's activities. "Sometimes I find her cryin in her room," I said. "I know she misses my grampa a lot."

"Ah, that's too bad about Mr. Roche. He was a keeper." Mrs. Flynn flipped the sausage patties with the spatula and reached over to the other pan to push the eggs around.

"Yes, Ma'am," I said. Spud shook his head.

"Enough already, Ma, huh? Leave 'im alone. You gave 'im the third degree already, yesterday." He shook his head some more. "He knows his grampa's dead and he knows his gramma lives with him, and you know that too." The two fixed their eyes on each other.

"It's okay," I said.

"See," Mrs. Flynn said. She knotted her arms across her chest and poked her tongue at Spud. Spud returned the favor. "Your grandmother been back to the old country lately?" she asked. Spud muttered something to himself and then stuffed his face in his cereal. I looked up from my tea to answer. Mrs. Flynn, busily tending to my breakfast, was poking into her nose with the edge of her thumb. She then dug in further. Several flakes broke lose from her nasal hairs and drifted down into the sausage pan. I stared at the pan with the sausage and nose flakes in it and failed to answer. Mrs. Flynn pointed her face back at me.

"Has she?" she asked.

"Has she what?" I was momentarily lost. It wasn't every day you saw a friend's mom diggin for boogers and then sprinkling them like seasoning over your breakfast meat.

"Gone back to Ireland?"

"Oh, my grandmother. No, no, she hasn't, but I think she's going next year."

"Grand, grand." I watched her. Mrs. Flynn dug in again and made a few more flakes coast down upon the sausage. The eggs in the other pan remained free from the booger assault. She turned both burners off.

"Here, you go, Dennis." Mrs. Flynn pushed the eggs onto my plate and plopped the three sausage patties next to them. She gave Spud two pieces of toast, already buttered. When she turned to get my toast, Mr. Flynn walked into the kitchen. He was clad in his work jeans, the kind with the hammer-loop on the side.

"What's for breakfast?" he said.

"I didn't cook anything for you yet."

"I sure as hell smell something," Mr. Flynn said. Spud kept his face in his cereal. I pushed the sausage to the rim of my plate and cut into my eggs. It was quiet for a moment. Then Mr. Flynn spoke.

"Who's dis one now?"

"You remember Dennis, the Roches' grandson." From the corner of my eye I saw Mr. Flynn reach for a newspaper on that same old, stained two-seater couch.

"Dennis Foley?" he said.

"Yes," she said.

"Tis him, isn't it. I never forget the nosy ones."

"Sean, stop," Mrs. Flynn said.

"Yah, Dad," said Spud. I didn't hear much of what they said next. I just stared at the breakfast on my plate. I had to do something and be nice about it, too. Especially with you-know-who there.

"Mrs. Flynn," I said, "I'm not a breakfast sausage kinda guy. I hope ya don't mind but I'm just gonna eat the eggs and toast. Okay?"

"That's just fine, Dennis."

"No it's not," the old man said. "Good food shouldn't go to waste."

For the first time in my life, I was overjoyed to see old man Flynn and hear him speak. His words gave me an idea. "I didn't touch it Mr. Flynn." He glared at me. “Honest, I didn't. And you're right. The sausage shouldn't go to waste. Here, you have it.” I lifted my plate and aimed it at him.

"You sure you didn't nibble on it?"

"Sure."

"Cuz I don't want to catch whatever it is you're carryin." He laughed to himself. "Okay. Fine. Give it here." I pushed the sausage onto the small plate he held in his hand.

Spud and I finished our breakfast at the same time and left for the basement. I turned back from the stairwell and watched and smiled as Mr. Flynn swallowed a huge chunk of his booger-flaked sausage. Cat-killing, mother-fucker," I breathed to myself as we hit the basement stairs.

Breakfast With Dad

The night of the big fight started like most any other Saturday night. I met the boys up on the front steps of Hubbard, where we gathered our dollars together, and then me and Bobby shoved off to get the beer. It was 8:00 pm, a chilly May night--jacket weather--and a full moon chased us as we walked.

"This Mendoza guy's a pretty bad dude, huh?" Bobby said as we made our way to Armanetti's.

"Yah, I'd say so." Last weekend I threw the hooks with Mendoza and he got the best of me. Fact is, and I aint proud sayin it, he beat the everlivin snot outta me. And I felt bad about that too--real bad. That was the first fight I'd ever lost. Mendoza's a big guy--had me by about 40 or 50 pounds--and he wore big army boots. And those boots were well oiled and black--just like his floppy-ass fro. It's those boots that did me in. My ribs were still achin. But this was a new night. This was the night we we're gonna meet Mendoza and all his boys. This wasn't gonna be no one-on-one shit, like last week. Sure Bobby and Mendoza would have center stage--our best against their best--but we were all gonna have a chance to have some fun. I was glad Bobby was here. He missed out on last week's fight. He was up in Michigan for some goofball relative's wedding.

"Is he quick with his hands?" Bobby asked.

"Nah," I said as I wagged my head. "I got some goods punches in on him. He didn't do shit with his fists." I rubbed my rib cage, letting my fingers trace the bruises through my jacket. My chest was home to a dozen or so tiny discolored, purple and blue mountains. I stopped walking and lifted up my jacket and my shirt to let Bobby have a look. He stared.

"Just watch out for those boots," I said. "They're heavy man. Real heavy. And don't let him get you down. That's when he got me good." I dropped my shirt and jacket back in place.

Bobby nodded his head. "Don't worry none," I added. "You can take 'im." Bobby nodded his head some more.

We caught a quick run at Armanetti's. Spud's oldest brother was heading in, so he picked up our beer for us. He's a decent guy, even though Spud says he a little bit too much of a "goody two shoes" for his liking. We didn't see a single cop on the way back. Thank God for dark alleys. When we made it back to Hubbard, we decided to move offa the porch cuz too many passerbys were eyeballin us. We figured one of 'em would call the cops. We found a spot in the alley behind St. Nick's school, and it was a great spot too. Some 8th grade kids were already there, drinkin their own beer. We ran 'em off and kept their beer.

"Double up, guys," Spud said. We all laughed cuz Spud was right. Instead of the usual 6 to 8 beers a guy, there was room for plenty more. There wasn't a whole lotta talk after that. We just shot-gunned and chugged our beers, gettin our minds and bodies ready for what they needed to do--ready to fight. And we have rules when we fight, ya know. We do. Sure we fight dirty, but still we have a code: fists, feet and teeth only. No weapons. Problem was: Mendoza was different, only I didn't know that until it was too late.

An hour and a half after we went into that alley, we came out--ready to kick some tail. And boy was I ready. I had a twelve pack in me. The rest of the boys had their fill, too. Bobby, Spud, Harry, Marty and Danny O, Finn and me were ready. We swung back past Hubbard to see who was there. Another handful of guys came along to join in the fun. I didn't know it at that time, but within ten minutes I would be having a dream--a death dream. But before the dream, there was reality.

We walked down the alley that separated 62nd Street from 62nd Place til it dead-ended at the tracks at Central Park. Mendoza was already there. So were his toy soldiers. This fight was a long time comin. Like I said--our best against their best, Manno y Manno. The alley became the ring and we, the onlookers, became the ropes, stationed around Bobby and Mendoza--our arms hooked together. The lone eye of a rust-covered street light flickered above us, giving off scattered spurts of light. Bobby wasted no time. He immediately tore into Mendoza with a series of right hooks. He clubbed him at least six times. A shoe to the balls dumped Mendoza to the concrete.

"The fucker's got a broken nose," Spud screeched. "Look at it. The fucker's broken." I kept my arms locked to the guys on both sides of me, but I pushed in to get a good look at that nose. Bobby had Mendoza face-down on the cement. He dropped a knee in his back and then, with both hands on Mendoza's fro, yanked his head and neck back over his shoulders. Mendoza was starin straight ahead. Our eyes met. I laughed. Spud was right. Mendoza's nose was curved to the right like the blade on a hockey stick. Blood fell out of it, thick as oil, onto the pavement. It was over then, and Mendoza knew it--only Bobby didn't know it yet. He jumped up and then slammed away at Mendoza's ribs with his feet. He was givin Mendoza a payback for what he did to me.

"How's that feel mother fucker? Huh? Huh?" Bobby kept swingin those feet and each time a kick landed, Mendoza flopped like a fish and then tried to cover up. "You like it mother fucker, huh? Tell me how it feels." Then Bobby dropped two final, heavy kicks to Mendoza's head.

The fight was now definitely over and I wasn't disappointed. Mendoza rolled about on the cement, his frame long and erect, his hands glued to his face. I stared at Bobby's white Con's as he circled Mendoza. Speckles of red in various sizes and shapes crawled across the white, canvass shoe, forming a hard-earned piece of art of sorts. Yep, it was over--way over. Only, I didn't want it over. Not just yet. It was then that the twelve Old Styles in charge of my brain spoke to me. "It aint over," the brew said. "It's just startin."

I pulled my arms free of the others and grabbed this kid, Mullins, by his long, red locks. He was standin right across from me, and I never liked the kid. How stupid, I thought as I smashed his face into a garage door, my hands still tearin at his mane. I stopped for a brief moment to check out the others. Everyone now had someone in their grips. Twelve on twelve. Our jury against their jury. I felt a strange sense of peace, an inner calm.

"Long hair has no place in alley fights, you stupid shit," I screamed into Mullins's ear. Then I flattened his nose with my knee. "You lose the advantage." And I believed what I said, too. That's why I kept my hair at Marine length. No one could use it against me. Then it came to me. The picket fence. Yah, the picket fence. Perfect. I dragged Mullins across the alley to the picket fence that ran along the alley, behind the Riley house. Old man Riley's house, itself, was nothin more than a tar-paper shanty, but for some odd reason, he always kept his pickets dressed with a fresh coat of white paint. I threw Mullins atop the fence. His feet and arms dangled on opposite sides of the pickets. He was my very own personal rag doll. I raised my arms above my head and locked my hands together. I brought my weapon down solidly upon Mullins's back. He screeched and then his arms and legs kicked out like a spaz. Again I raised my arms. One more blow oughta bust open his ribs, I figured. Yes indeedy, one more blow oughta do it. But before I delivered that blow, I felt something enter my back, and then everything started to move in slow motion. I turned and saw Mendoza running from me, his frizzy black hair bouncing as he moved. He was putting distance between us, but yet he seemed to be running in place. Why are you runnin in place, you dumb ass? How come you can't move, you stupid shit? These questions flashed through my brain. I wanted to ask them but my lips wouldn't move. For some strange reason, they were sewn shut. Just then, a siren screamed and I looked around for a squad car. I couldn't see the lights. But no one else was looking for the squad. Just me. The fighting stopped. Everyone was now staring at me--staring, just staring--like crows gettin ready to rip into some fresh road-kill. Even my own friends--staring, just staring. I wanted to scream, but my lips still wouldn't work.

The car that made the noise finally raced down the alley, blue lights blazing. It was only then that I regained a few moments of speed. The alley cleared in seconds. Bodies hurdled fences, broke into garages, and dashed the length of the alley like Olympic sprinters. I made it all of fifteen feet. I flipped old man Riley's picket fence and started to run. But after a few steps I collapsed into Mrs. Riley's perennial garden, grabbing hold of a fiery Maltese Cross as I melted into the dirt.

* * * * *

I was out cold once I hit those flowers. Bobby and Spud found me. They dragged me over to the next block and put me in the O'Gradys' car. With all of them inside, Marty O' raced me over to Holy Cross Hospital. I remember none of the ride or anything after that. All I remember is the dream. I can still see it plain as day.

I don't know where I am. I hear voices all around me but I see nothin. Everything is hazy, a dense fog surrounds me. I later learn that that was when I was on the operating table. Mendoza's blade dealt the damage he wanted. It was my time. My number was up, as they say. The fog clears swiftly as though it was never there. A clock starts ticking. I can hear every single movement of the second hand. But where is that clock? Someone tell me. Please! I need to know what time it is. I don't know why. I just need to know the time. The ticks from the clock turn into buzzing. Colors flash before me--reds, greens, yellows, oranges--buzzing as they come and go. My eyes dart about but still I see nothin--nothin but those colors. That buzzing sound is still here. I know there's a swarm of bees somewhere around here. But I can't find 'em. Then I see the light, the light, ah yes--the light. Yes--it is my time. I know it now. The light is a magnet pulling me gently toward it like a mother pulling a newborn softly to her breast. I am in a tunnel now. You should see it. Everything is moving so slow. I feel so good. I could probably dunk a basketball now if I tried. I move closer to the light and the closer I get, the better I feel. I am tumbling and flying, bouncing off the invisible wall of my tunnel. God, I love it. I don't want to leave this place, ever.

Finally, the light is upon me. I am at the end of the tunnel. There is a hole there. Tiny beams of light fill up my fingertips, and parts of me start to glow. I reach an arm up and am about to pull myself out of my tunnel. But I can't get myself out. Someone is pulling on my leg, yanking me away from the light. Let go of me, I try to scream, but my lips still don't work. After one final, strong pull, I fall from my tunnel and land at Wrigley Field in the outstretched arms of my dead father. He sits me down next to him. We're sitting in the center field bleachers, the shadow from the scoreboard upon us. We stare out at the field watching a game not being played.

"What did ya do that for, Dad?" I ask.

"What?" he says.

"You know what," I say through twisted lips. "That was the best darn feeling I ever had and you ruined it. You always ruin—"

"Look," my father says, pointing towards home plate, "Ernie's up." I look out at the field. The bright green blades of grass bow as Mr. Cub, Ernie Banks, wanders to the plate, the bat that whacked over 500 homers dangling from his shoulder. Ernie steps into the box and digs a small hole with his right foot, scraping his metal cleats into the dirt over and over again. He finally plants that foot, and then the left foot, and readies for the pitch. He points his bat like a lance in the direction of the pitcher. Problem is, there's no pitcher on the mound. Ernie's pointin' at us.

"How do ya want your eggs, scrambled or fried?" my father asks. I'm still watchin Ernie and barely hear my father's words. Then, with a puff of magician's smoke, Ernie vanishes from sight. I turn and look at my father. He has a skillet in his right hand and a I'm-tired-of-waitin-on-ya look on his face.

"Scrambled, I guess," I finally say, scratching my head.

"Wheat or white toast?" he barks.

"Since when did you become a waiter?" My father says nothing. The skillet is now burning brightly atop the green bleacher. My eggs bubble in the pan. My father has a pencil and order pad in hand, staring at me. His mouth is still closed. I don't find this unusual. He almost never answered any of my questions while he was alive, so why should he answer my questions now? But I quickly grow tired of the silence. I give in.

"White," I say as plainly as the toast I will assuredly soon receive. My father checks the watch on his left wrist. His face shudders as though he has forgotten something--or remembered something. He tosses away the skillet. It bounces atop the bleachers, catapulting my meal as it moves, until it rests in the wire basket at the wall. I can't find my eggs or toast anywhere, though I work the aisles like a frantic beer vendor on a steamy July day.

"You have to go back," my father commands.

"No Dad," I say, "I wanna stay here. Lemme stay here with you."

"You can't. We're not ready for you yet."

"Please Dad, let me stay with you." I am begging now, begging like a little boy who wants a toy at the store. "I just wanna be with you, Dad. That's all I've ever wanted." My father grabs me and starts pushing me into a hole. But it's more than a hole. It's a sewer. I can see the man-hole cover just a few feet away. I refuse to go. I push back against my father. But no matter how hard I push, he doesn't budge. He is stronger than me. I am losing the battle.

"I love you Dad," I yell. My father says nothing. He kicks at me with his right foot instead. "You never said you loved me. Do you love me, Dad?" My father steps on my fingers. "Say it, Dad. Just say it," I yell as tears finally claim my eyes. I drop into the hole and my father kicks the man-hole cover in place. Through the grate I see parts of my father's body--the bottom of a shoe, the cuffs on his pants, his golden hair atop his head. He is now giant-like. He stoops down and eyes me through the grate, bobbing his head about to find my face. He is crying.

"I DO love you son. More than you'll ever know. I'm just so sorry I never told you before." His giant tears fall into the sewer. It fills quickly. The tears swim up to my neck. If much more comes, I know I will drown. But I don't care. My father loves me and I am going to drown in the tears that are the proof of his love. Snap! I am gone. Wrigley Filed is no more, nor is my father. For an instant, I am floating in a river of Maltese Crosses, the red buds soft to touch and pleasant to smell. Snap! I awake. I come to in a hospital bed, a tube dangling from my side. I see something pass before me, approaching me. I focus my eyes and find a young nurse at my side. She smiles at me and races from the room, her tight buns bouncing as she moves, and I knew then that I was alive. And then the pain comes and comes and comes. I feel the holes in my chest. One made by Mendoza and one by the doctor.

Holy Cross Hospital--Day 10

I'm going home later tonight. Yippee. I'm glad to be leaving this place. But in a strange way, I'm sad. I've met some nice people here, and I've done a lot of thinkin. But one thing I haven't really thought about is just how lucky I am to be alive, how close I came to gettin planted. I know I'm lucky. My dad helped get me a second chance, a second life. He stopped me from climbing out of that feel-good tunnel. Somehow, someway, he did it. He came through for me. I am convinced of that.

Visitors. The boys are finally here. Yippee. Harry, Bobby, Spud and Finn are in my room. The twins are workin with their old man. When the nurse leaves, Harry closes the door. He pulls some Old Styles from his coat pocket. Bobby does the same. They crack their beers open and tell me how good it is to see me and how lucky I am. I agree. Then Harry asks do I want a beer.

I think and then I look at them. I know I shouldn't have a beer. I know it with absolute certainty. But their faces want me to have a beer. Their faces want me not to be any different. And then a strange thing happens--faces and snapshots dart before me. But these are not faces from the past. I see myself in college, 20 and smiling. I see myself married and with my kids. I see my face at 35, worried. More snapshots, more faces flash past, but then slip away. I blink my eyes and shake my head and look back at Harry. He's still holding out a beer, smiling, aiming it in my direction. The future is so far off, so far away. This is here. This is now. I smile at my friends and say, Sure, I'll take one. I snap open the Old Style and take a good long swig. The boys smile and give me a few Atta Boys. And so I drink my beer and look deeply into the smiling eyes of my friends, their cans pressed to their lips. The sun sneaks through a crack in the curtains and aims its interrogating rays upon my face. Again I am filled with thoughts of the future and I try hard to stop them. But now I can't. I look back at my friends and all I can do is wonder, what will become of us? What will become of me?

ABOUT THE AUTHOR

A lifelong Chicagoan, Dennis Foley's short stories, memoir pieces and freelance work have appeared in a number of literary venues including *HairTrigger, Poetry Motel, The Use of Personal Narratives in the Helping Profession, The Chicago Red Streak,The2ndHand, Gravity,* and centerstagechicago.com.

Dennis' first book, *The Street's and San Man's Guide To Chicago Eats*, won the Midwest Independent Publishers Association Book Awards—1st Place for Humor. Foley holds an MFA in Creative Writing from Columbia College-Chicago and a J.D. from The John Marshall Law School. He currently teaches English and coaches lacrosse at his alma mater, St. Laurence High School in Burbank, Illinois. Over the years, Foley has held numerous jobs including: bouncer, beer line cleaner, prosecutor, criminal defense attorney, electrician, dog walker, newspaper deliveryman, teacher, and coach. Happily married to Susan, Dennis is also the proud father of Matt, Pat, and Mike.